MW00509918

## Table of Contents

# Introduction:

Most people were not familiar with Bitcoin when it was initially released in the year 2009. But as of now, Bitcoin is the most popular type of cryptocurrency available in the world. This decentralized digital currency gained a lot of value over the years and increased a lot in value compared to its value in the beginning.

Most people still are confused about the concepts of Blockchain, Cryptocurrency, and specifically Bitcoin. Even though some people are enthusiastic to know everything about Bitcoin, they find it hard because of the comprehensive terminology used by experts to describe it.

For example, let us say that Bitcoin is a form of cryptocurrency that has been verified by network nodes with the help of cryptography and is recorded in a public ledger known as a blockchain. You might find it extremely hard to understand.

This is because you might not be familiar with cryptography or blockchain. By hearing this, some of you might be thinking like "Who doesn't know about cryptography or blockchain?". Trust us, some people might not be familiar with terms like cryptography or blockchain for various reasons.

The concept of Bitcoin might even sound like 'Rocket Science' to some people, whereas it is not. To understand it, you just need to have some interest in the topic and a little bit of patience (enough to read this book). Therefore, with the help of firm determination, we have decided to tell everything about Bitcoin in an exciting way so that you will not have any difficulty in having a better understanding of this concept.

To provide you extensive knowledge on this topic, we also included some other topics. Some topics like Blockchain, Cryptocurrency, etc., will help you get familiar with Bitcoin, while some other topics will help you store Bitcoin or invest in Bitcoin. Not only subjects, but we also included as many examples as we can to describe every single term related to our discussion.

As that has been said, let us waste no more time and take a dive into our book that concentrates on every aspect of bitcoin. So, hoping that you are ready, let's begin the process of knowing everything about Bitcoin.

If you are a beginner and have truly little to no knowledge on this topic, we highly recommend that you stay in the loop from the beginning.

If you have intermediate-level knowledge about Bitcoin, you can get more experience on this topic by knowing all the details mentioned in this book.

If you are an advanced cryptocurrency trader/miner, well, it is beneficial to know everything about the topic once again. In a simple sentence, we want to suggest to you to read everything mentioned without skipping it.

# **Chapter 1**

# What is money?

Before we get to know what exactly a Bitcoin or a Cryptocurrency is, we need to be familiar with the concept and nature of money. This will be helpful as Bitcoin, which is a Cryptocurrency, is also a form of money. Therefore, knowing the nature of money will help you in understanding the nature of Cryptocurrencies as well. By doing so, you will also understand the details of money.

In very basic terms, money is an object that is used to represent and determine the value of other items. For example, let us assume if you went to a Gas Station for filling gas. You wanted to fill a gallon of gas and a gallon of gas costs around $2.50. Then, you would pay $2.50 for getting a gallon of gas. Here, the money of $2.5 you are paying is the value you compensated for getting a gallon of gas. The gas station owner would use that money to acquire something that is of the same value. In this way, cash keeps revolving around people while changing hands.

If we take back a look at the history, there have been many sorts of money. Even before these types of money, there used to be a system called Barter System. To understand the barter system, let us take a look at an example. Imagine that there are two persons, namely A and B. A has fruits with him, while B has some vegetables with him. Then, A wants to have vegetables, while B wants to have fruits. What they do is exchange the items they have and get what they want. However, it is not an ideal system. If A did not want to have vegetables, but B wanted to have fruits, then both of them won't be able to get what they want.

The barter system was replaced with different money types in the later centuries, which ranged from stones, seashells, food items (like wheat), salt, gold, etc. As an evolution of these first-ever created forms, money was made, which we use today.

# Chapter 2
# Reason for Evolution (to Paper Money)

Yes, Money had evolved a lot since there was a time when wheat or salt was used. This was not way too many centuries ago. To be more precise, this was just two centuries ago. So, why did people want to evolve in the way they make use of money? Why didn't they just stick with the traditional wheat or salt, which they preferred as a medium of money? If you are also thinking the same, excellent question. Well, we got the perfect answer for you.

For this, we will observe a perfect example of the actual reason for the evolution. Take wheat into consideration, as money, as an example. Let's just say that for a bag of grain, you'll get enough groceries for five days. If you wanted to buy enough groceries for a month, you would have to pay with six bags of wheat. Similarly, if you wanted to have groceries for six months, you would have to pay 36 bags of grain. So, how exactly are you going to take those 36 bags of wheat to the shop? If 100 people thought in the same way as you did and wanted to have groceries for six months, the shop owner would receive 3600 bags of wheat. Where is he going to store all that wheat? What if rodents became a huge problem and most of the grain had been eaten by them? If inflation occurred and the price of six bags became twelve bags, what would you do with all that excessive wheat? How will you or the shop owner transport all that wheat? What if there was heavy rain and all the grain was damaged?

Very inconvenient, right? That is why people had to evolve in how they choose their money and opted for something more effective against such problems. That led our ancestors to invent paper money, which is an efficient form of money.

There used to be certificates or bills, which were used to represent money in the very beginning. For example, if you had some gold and let the government have possession of your gold physically. Then, the government will issue you a $1000 certificate/bills (whatever the gold was worth) for the gold you deposited with them.

Now let's think of it this way, would you rather carry a few bars of gold, or would you carry papers that are worth your gold? What is a more convenient way for you? Exactly! So, with these bills, you could buy whatever you would like to purchase. For example, you wanted to grab a beer, and the beer costs $5. You would then pay $5 worth of bills from the $1000 issued to you earlier. Instead, if you had $1000 worth of gold, how will you be able to cut a piece out of it that would exactly be worth $5? Yes, that's very tricky.

What if you wanted to take possession of your gold from the government again (which had been deposited earlier)? It's simple; you just need to pay $1000 to the bank or government that issued you $1000 worth of bills or certificates. Simple as that. This convenience led people to opt for paper money, which was very efficient compared to other forms of money. As of today, paper money is the most common form of money used anywhere in the world.

In the olden days, the value of the United States dollar was linked to gold's value. The entire money that the United States had in its possession depended on the amount of gold owned by the country. There is an actual term for this, which was called the 'Gold Standard'. As the years passed, as the country's macroeconomy experienced a change, this connection between gold and the US dollar value changed. This resulted in the US dollar becoming the world's primary currency, and instead of being dependent on gold, it is now dependent on the Federal Government.

To describe it in simpler terms, people have shifted their faith in money to something materialistic like gold to somebody they trust, i.e., the Federal government. The main reason for this monetary value system being dependent on the government to continue is trust. Now, there is no underlying asset that is responsible for the monetary value of the US dollar or any other currency, for that matter. This explains the evolution of money to Fiat Money.

# Chapter 3
# Currency

Currency is nothing but money, which a government issues within its areas of jurisdiction. Generally, it exists in the form of paper or coins and is accepted as a payment method depending on its face value.

In other words, the currency is nothing but money, and it is different for each country. For example, the US currency is the dollar, while the UK's currency is GBP. The value of a currency is volatile, and the value of that currency keeps continually changing with respect to other countries' money in the world. The currency exchange market, also known as the Foreign Exchange market, is where people can benefit from these fluctuations.

In most countries, US Dollar is accepted as a means of payment, while some other countries base their currency value on the US Dollar. In the modern days, our world has entered a new era with virtual currency, which is neither backed by the government nor has a physical existence. We will get to that part after some time; meanwhile, we will take a look at the term Fiat Money.

**Coins -** Each country has its own type of currency used in that specific country. As for the kinds of money, we will just start with coins first. Coins are the currency that has been in existence for a while now. A few centuries ago, coins had a face value depending on the metal that has been used to make that coin. At first, silver coins came into existence as a form of currency, followed by gold coins. After some decades, bronze was also added to the list of metals that were used to make coins. But, slowly, after some time has passed, people chose metals considered non-precious metals, such as copper.

Usually, these metals were mined, weighed, and then made into coins. In this way, there would be an exact estimation of how much these coins weighed and their value. However, coins could be replicated initially, but later on, they could be tested for their authenticity even when they were shaved, or wore off, or were tampered with.

In the olden times, most of the more prominent countries were using coinage, which had several tiers of coins. Each type of coin among these tiers had different face values. For instance, if we look at coins made from gold, silver, and copper. Gold coins were used for valuable purchases and were considered expensive. These were often paid to officials and some other government (state/country) related activities. Silver coins would be used for making medium-sized transactions. Meanwhile, copper coins were used for everyday use. Historians observed this system, which has been explained as an example in ancient India.

When it came to the value of coins in ancient times, the rarity of the metal was responsible for the coin's monetary value. Gold was rare compared to silver, and it was very pricey, and silver was valuable compared to metals like bronze or copper. Nowadays, coins are used as a fraction of the actual paper money that is being used. For example, In the United States, we have coins, namely 1¢, 5¢, 10¢, 50¢, and even $1. These have a monetary value less than a dollar bill (except for the $1 coin). Some bullion coins are produced with the help of precious metals such as Gold, Silver, and Platinum. Since 2017, there is even availability of a Palladium coin.

In most current-day scenario scenarios, coins have a monetary value less than that of paper currency. One of the main reasons for this is that people can't make more significant transactions using coins easily. They can do those transactions using notes. Imagine if you wanted to complete a transaction of 1 million dollars. How easy would it be if it is done with paper money? You can just fill a million dollars in a briefcase with $1000 bills, and it will not be difficult. Specifically, it will not be nearly as difficult as gathering 50¢ or $1 coins worth $1 million. Adding to that, how much time would it take to count all those coins? Yeah, we understand.

**Paper Money** – Paper Money is much easier to carry around or pay when compared to pay in coins or carrying money in coins. The early 7th to 12th century was the time when most of the earliest paper currencies were invented. In countries like China and Islamic countries started printing paper money that was of high monetary value. This made it possible for them to conduct high-value transactions very conveniently. By the time we reached the 1900s, most modern-day countries got used to paper money, even some of them were dependent on the theory of gold standard. The last country that left the gold standard was the United States, which was achieved in 1971, referred to as the 'Nixon Shock". Currently, no country in the world still follows the gold standard or silver standard.

# Chapter 4
# Inflation

Before we know what Fiat Money is, let us look at inflation and various types of it, which will come in handy for having an in-depth analysis of the problems caused by fiat money. Boring but important for the eventual creation of Bitcoin.

**Inflation** – Inflation is a situation where the purchasing power of a currency gets decreased over time. Due to this, we might observe an increase in the price of goods and services over that period of time (when inflation occurs). If we follow closely, the products you buy or services you acquire were slightly less pricey than their current prices. This is an apt example to describe inflation. Over time, everything you buy, every service you receive will have an increase in the price. Even the haircut you get from your barber will not be of the same price in the next few years.

In the United States, inflation has resulted in a decrease in the value of the United States Dollar compared to what it was in the past. Inflation usually results in a higher cost of living as time goes on. President Ronald Reagan uniquely stated inflation. He said that inflation was as violent as a mugger, frightening as a robber, and deadly as a hitman. In order to deal with inflation, the Federal Reserve makes use of the monetary policy. People like you and me can keep inflation in check if we can make some good investments and follow some tips. As a bonus, we will also provide you some tips to cope with inflation in a few moments.

The percentage used to represent the increase or decrease in inflation is known as the Inflation Rate. This percentage helps understand how much inflation is occurring. If there is an inflation rate of 2% per year, you might experience the prices of goods and services increasing 2% every year. For example, if 1 liter of milk costs you $1 and the inflation is 2%, it would cost you $1.20 next year because of the inflation of 2%.

There are various types of scenarios regarding inflation. Let's take a peek into each of those without going too deep into the details of those terms.

- Inflation ranging up to 3%

Also known as mild inflation, the inflation that is 3% or less indicates that the country is on the right track. The country that is experiencing inflation that is 2% or low is generally on the right path to achieve economic growth. However, people in a country with inflation having around 3% would generally be expecting the prices to go upward because of a general boost in demand. There are chances that people might excessively buy the products now so that they do not have to pay higher prices in the future. As for this general reason, mild inflation becomes a factor of economic expansion. To have perfect economic growth within the US, the feds keep 2% of inflation as a target.

- Inflation of 3% to 10%

This sort of inflation is somewhat impactful and quite effective than what we discussed previously. This is dangerous for an economy as the economy gets heated up too fast because of this. Forget chances; people will buy more goods to avoid paying hefty prices in the future. This resulted increase in the prices of goods will consistently result in an increase in the demand. Because of an increase in demand, the suppliers of goods and services might not be able to keep up with the supply.

As the respective goods and services become scarce, the prices of those goods and products surge. Adding to that, people's wages remain the same, which reduces their ability to afford the goods and services. Finally, the situation worsens, and ordinary people will not be able to afford most of the goods and services.

- Inflation of more than 10%

This is a rapid form of inflation, where the inflation rate exceeds 10% in a year. This has an extreme impact on the economy and the lives of the people living in it. Money loses its value within a short period of time. Many companies close their businesses, and people cannot buy goods and services (even things related to daily needs). By understanding the scenario, even foreign investors lose their interest in that country. When foreign investors are not going to invest, the country lacks the capital needed. The economy becomes unsteady beyond predictability. This type of inflation should be prevented at any cost.

- Hyperinflation

Hyperinflation is something we can call with many names, such as disaster, tragedy, calamity, and many more. Hyperinflation is the worst situation that can happen within an economy. In this sort of inflation, the inflation rate exceeds 50% a month (or a specific period). Remember the liter of milk we bought for $1? The hyperinflation situation would be increased to $1.5 next month and $2 in the later month, and finally, it would become $7 by the end of the year. Yes, it is a disaster. A general situation that might lead to hyperinflation is the government's printing of excessive amounts of money for funding wars. There have been instances when some countries experienced hyperinflation. Even the United States experienced hyperinflation during the time of civil war.

- Stagflation

Stagflation is the type of situation where a country's economy remains motionless, yet inflation occurs. Most people might think of this concept to be impossible, but it is not. You might be wondering why there would be a surge in the prices even if there is no increase in demand for goods and services? Well, let us take a look at a situation where stagflation happened and what the government of that economy did to keep that in check.

It was around the 1970s. This was the time when the United States decided to cast aside the gold standard. As soon as the link between gold and cash came to an end, the value of money took a drastic fall, and gold's price experienced a tremendous surge. This continued until 1979, when the chairman of Federal Reserve Paul Volcker started to take the necessary measures. He then targeted the interest rates and raised the prime lending rate to more than 20 percent, and because of that, the dollar rate became depreciated. After facing two recessions, the value was finally stabilized.

- Core Inflation

Core inflation is the term when inflation of everything is taken into accountability except for food and energy. "What is the connection between gas and food and Why Gas and not anything else?".

Usually, gas prices tend to have an increase in the summer of every year. There are a few reasons for this, but the fundamental reason is because of vacation. Usually, families go out for vacation trips during summer, increasing gas prices. Also, the summer heat is another major factor. As the price of gas increases, everything that needs to be transported will also increase in price.

Henceforth, food and other things that need transportation also increase. The federal reserve system does not want to increase the interest rates every time there is a hike in gas prices. Therefore, it opts for core inflation in order to set the monetary policy.

- Deflation

As the term suggests, the exact opposite of inflation is called deflation. Deflation is another major issue that needs just as much attention as inflation. Deflation occurs when the prices of assets drop at a faster pace. This is the exact situation that happened in the year 2006. Deflation of the houses' prices became a significant burden. The people who bought those houses in 2005 were trapped. The federal reserve system was worried a great deal about this situation as deflation would generally lead to recession and finally result in depression. When the depression occurred in 1929, which is known as the Great Depression of 1929, the prices dropped at a rate of 10% each year. Like hyperinflation, deflation can be an extreme scenario that cannot be contained easily.

-    Wage Inflation

Yes, when there is inflation regarding wages called Wage Inflation. This is when the wages of workers increase a lot with respect to the cost of living. For example, let us assume that an average worker earns around $5,000 per month, and the expenses related to the cost of living of that person are $2,500. So, when wage inflation happens, the cost of living remains the same $2,500 while the earnings of that person increase (let's say $6,000 or $7,000).

There are three main reasons for this type of inflation to occur. The first one is a shortage of workers. Second, when labor unions negotiate with the companies for higher wages. Ultimately, the last reason is when workers have control over their pay.

Most people might think that the increase in people's wages is a necessary evil, but it can eventually lead to cost-push inflation and result in the prices of a company's goods and services. As it is a familiar doubt that "Why would an increase in the wages lead to a hike in the prices of goods and services?", well… we will explain why.

When a company is required to pay more wages to their employees, they consider this into their production expenses. They add the amount given out to the employees into the price of goods and services to maintain profits. Usually, this will become a cycle. You know why? When a company sells its goods and services at a higher price in order to maintain profits, the employees/labor will again ask for an increase in their wages as the company is performing well (in their opinion). Then, the company would also have to increase the prices of their goods and services due to an increase in production cost. When people could even get the slightest idea of what is happening, this whole situation turns out into a wage-price spiral and goes merry-go-round.

-    Asset Inflation

Asset Inflation. The name itself is going to give you a general idea about what this inflation actually means. Yes, you are right! This is related to assets. However, it is not just limited to a single type of asset. Instead, this type of inflation occurs in various asset classes. Let us see some of the assets in which asset inflation could generally be observed.

Gas – As discussed before, gas prices have a surge in the summer in the United States. This is primarily due to most people wanting to travel a lot during summer, specifically for a vacation. Anyhow, impact in the oil-exporting countries can also become a major contributing factor for the rise in gasoline prices. To be more precise, the oil prices are responsible for more than 66% of the gas price, while the remaining is based on the distribution and taxes.

Oil – Crude Oil had the highest price during the time of the economic crisis of 2008. It was estimated that a barrel of crude had a hefty price of $145.31 in July 2008. As most of you might think, there was no excessive demand for crude oil during that time. In fact, there was a decrease in the global demand as well as an increase in the supply. Commodities traders are the people who determine the prices of oil. They can either be speculators or corporate traders that are hedging the risk factor faced by them. In general, traders expect to increase oil prices when the supply is threatened or when the demand becomes more.

Food – This can be considered the most common type of inflation observed in various parts of the world and will repeat again. An increase in the prices of food is the most predictable type of inflation. When this happens, food riots occur.

Gold – Gold, as most people know, is one of the precious metals available to us. Gold prices skyrocketed on September 5th of 2011 to a massive $1,895.

Most investors did not refer to this scenario as inflation, but it actually was. This increase in the price of gold had nothing to do with the demand or the supply.

This was because most people opted to invest in gold as they thought it would be the best type of investment for them to keep their money safe, more like a safe haven for their money. Most people panic when they observe a decline in the value of their currency. In such situations, they want to stay invested in an asset that is more likely to be profitable.

**Causes of Inflation** – In General, there are two leading causes for inflation to occur. The first and foremost reason is demand-pull inflation, whereas the second one is cost-push inflation.

Demand-pull inflation is when the demand for the specific type of goods and services increases while the supply becomes low that it cannot meet the demand.

Cost-push inflation is often rarely observed when compared to demand-pull inflation. This happens when suppliers face issues. When something impactful happens to the supply, the prices of the goods and services increase regardless of the demand.

One of the most important reasons that are known for causing inflation is the government printing out money excessively. This escalation in the money supply will lead to an increase in capital. Excessive capital will target very few goods and result in demand-pull inflation or cost-push inflation.

**How can it be managed?** – Central banks all over the world make use of monetary policy to avoid inflation as well as deflation. Some countries set a target rate for inflation and try to stay within that specific inflation rate over the specific time given.

Some countries evaluate inflation based on core inflation to rule out the inflation in the prices of certain goods and services, which are too volatile to be taken into consideration.

Some other countries try to achieve a target inflation rate of more than 2%. By doing so, they try to lower the unemployment within that economy. However, after successfully meeting their economic goals, these countries would again opt for having an inflation of 2%, which is optimistic for the growth and development of a nation.

**What should you do?** – One of the most efficient ways for you to deal with inflation is by increasing your earning potential and how much you earn. In general, a rise of around 5% every year or similar to that would be an excellent measure against inflation. If you are not able to achieve this, then there are some other alternatives for this.

The next best thing is investing in financial instruments such as stocks. However, certain types of investment vehicles carry many risks. It is highly suggested to have thorough research on the specific type of investment you are going to invest in. Additionally, it would be even more beneficial if you acquire a financial planner or an investment adviser's services.

There are some other alternatives to deal with inflation, such as TIPS (Treasury Inflated Protected Securities), Series I Bonds, etc.

When the chances are high for your economy will be experiencing hyperinflation, you might need to some more measures. First of all, you need to have a well-diversified portfolio. A well-diversified portfolio usually consists of a wide range of assets such as stocks, bonds, cryptocurrencies, real estate investments, and others. The balance should be maintained efficiently among these assets, and the strategy should be tailored in such a way that you can deal with any sort of consequences.

In case things go out of hand than what you have anticipated, make sure that you have a passport ready. In that way, you can move out of your country to avoid extreme situations and unimaginable and intolerable standards of living.

It might also be beneficial for you to be skilled in a specific aspect, whether it is a skill related to programming, designing, or anything that is considered a popular talent among other nations. In this way, even if you move out of your country, you might have a sustainable living regardless of the consequences. It might even help you find a new job faster if you have an extensive set of skills and unique talent.

# Chapter 5
# Fiat Money

**Fiat Money -** is a term used to represent money that the respective country's government backs. Both the coins and paper money used within a country could be called Fiat Money unless that country's government has not declared their value. The very meaning of 'Fiat' refers to 'by Decree', which clarifies that the value of this money is based on what the government decides its value to be.

There are approximately more than 180 fiat currencies in the world so far that are in circulation. Because fiat money is based on the legal decrees of value, it is also considered a legal tender, meaning any person who sells goods and services within a country should accept them as a payment mode. Money gains its value based on what a country's government declares its value to be. This is because people often prefer the value of money based on someone they can rely on (such as the government) rather than materialistic (such as gold). This theory has already been discussed earlier by us while we were discussing the evolution of money.

Some problems occur because of using fiat money, which might be considered serious issues. Fiat money is centralized and is technically unlimited in quantity. This means a government, or any other monetary authority has the full power to print money as much as they like. A question that might arise in most of you right now, which is, "How is printing excessive money going to be a problem?", well... because printing too much money will all most certainly lead to hyperinflation.
When the Federal Reserve or any other monetary authority for that matter prints too much money, the markets are lying within that country will be

flooded with that specific currency.

When something is available excessively, it loses its value. Similar is the case when it comes to printing out excessive amounts of money. So, when this happens, the prices of goods and services might not have a surge immediately. But the prices will skyrocket sooner or later. It does not mean that the goods and services have become more expensive. Instead, it means that the increased money supply became a reason for the decrease in money value.

So, what are some other problems that are to be faced because of fiat money? Well, let us see.

- Controlled by Central Government:

In most cases, the fiat currencies are based on coercion (which means forceful) instead of being voluntarily accepted. Then only will a central authority stay in control by eliminating the competing currencies and establish a monopoly?

- Coercion:

It is one of the significant issues faced because of fiat money and a contributing factor for fiat money. Because most people will not follow or accept such things unless they are forcefully needed to do so.

When the United States wanted to replace the gold standard in 1933, they made it a legally necessary measure to use it. People who did not wish to accept the new type of fiat currency were subject to penalties. As people became afraid of these penalties, they could not do anything but accept this new form of fiat money.

- Price Instability:

Fiat money needs a significant amount of unimportant physical as well as economic inputs to be produced. When there is no requirement for production, fiat currency's value will no longer have a direct relationship with the economic reality of the actual world.

Central authorities declare the value of fiat money, and because of that, the quantity of fiat currency will most probably be incorrect. This inaccuracy will lead to instability in the prices and stimulate or depress the economic activity of a country in an artificial way. This is a factor based on how much currency has been created and how this currency gets distributed. Eventually, it becomes awfully hard to reach stability in the prices because of the fiat currency.

- Economic Volatility:

Fiat currencies are not significantly linked to the physical or economic activity of the real world. Because of that, they will become dissociated and unbound with them (given the time). An economy comprises millions of individuals, and the people responsible for estimating the required quantity and distributing it will be able to determine the exact amount needed.

Even if they could speculate approximate quantities depending on the statistics and the consequences faced previously, inaccurate amounts of money will eventually increase credits, recessions, inflations, and even an economic collapse. Economies can be volatile for a handful of reasons, and these fiat currencies become a factor for the increase in economic volatility.

- Debasement:

Fiat currencies operate based on ethereal concepts such as faith in the central authority and credit. At the same time, there is no enduring value for the currency itself. A French writer named 'Voltaire' stated that paper money would come back to its intrinsic value in the end, which is zero. Additionally, fiat currencies tend to experience a decrease in purchasing power within a specific period of time because other currencies will be produced as time passes by. This can be observed more clearly in the cases of fractional reserve and debt-based fiat currencies.

When it comes to debt-based currencies, the currency would require inflation continuously. If not, there will be a severe case of deflation, which is as disastrous as high inflation, as we have discussed earlier. People with the authority to create these currencies will generate more than what is actually required. This has also been discussed previously, and we know what will happen when a currency gets printed excessively.

- Redistribution of Wealth:

When there is an increase in the money supply than that of what is needed in an economy, money distribution is distorted. The purchasing power is redistributed because of this distortion, which means the wealth from the rich will be taken and given to the poor in that economy. Production of wealth will generate overall net wealth in an economy, but wealth redistribution is quite the opposite. The economy would have to face a loss in overall wealth because of this redistribution scenario.

Deficiency in the government's spending will lead to alteration in the quantity of the currency and will finally result in currency debasement. When the government experiences a deficiency in its spending, people who save their money or work for wages will be subject to hidden taxes.

- The concentration of wealth:

Given the required amount of time, fiat money will make the people rich, who have access to creating that currency. This will lead to the concentration of wealth in that specific economy. When the concentration of wealth is extreme in an economy, the stability of that economy gets ruptured. This is because one individual having a significant income might not buy as many goods and services as ten individuals would buy when a large amount of wealth has been equally distributed among those ten people.

- Moral Risk:

Just because monetary authorities have the ability to create fiat currencies with the help of loan contracts, they offer a legal way of obtaining something valuable for absolutely nothing. Thus, the authorities responsible for making these currencies will have excessive power over that society's economic and political aspects.

There is no sustainable currency system that allows one specific group of individuals in a society to get something from nothing. The societies involved with this culture will develop an exceeding interest in it and lead to a situation where people would be living at the expense of other people instead of generating their own wealth.

- Conclusion on Fiat Currencies:

Finally, Fiat currencies act as a medium of exchange and depend on intangible things such as faith and confidence for determining the face value. As a result of this, the value of fiat money becomes extremely sensitive. It is subject to failure when the people of that economy lose their belief in that currency's intrinsic value. Fiat currencies are entirely reliant on the central monetary authorities and face debasement every now and then. The degeneration, as said before, will become a responsible factor for instability in the prices and economic volatility.

# Chapter 6
# Digital Money

**Digital Money –** Digital Money is also known by various names such as Digital Currency, Electronic Money, Electronic Currency, CyberCash, etc. As the name itself suggests the meaning of this, digital money is the type of money present in a digital form rather than having a physical presence. It is not a tangible asset like paper money or assets such as gold. Digital currency can be accessed with the help of electronic devices such as a computer, mobile phone, and others.

The foundation of fiat money made it easy to create digital money, even mandatory in some cases. Digital money came into existence in the 1990s (approx.), a very short time after the internet was invented. Many digital cash companies were formed during that period, but they were not able to sustain their businesses and went bankrupt.

The first-ever digital cash company that was familiar to most people was Digi Cash. Including that, most companies failed to operate as people found it hard to digest the concept of eCommerce and even the internet. Even though some retailers would accept digital money by that time, it did not gain much prominence. PayPal was the first digital cash company that gained wide popularity all over the world. It brought significance to the idea of making digital transactions.

Most financial services providers use digital money transfers and help with online money transactions between strangers or between people who are far away from each other. Without the help of digital money, most present-day companies would not see as many profits as they do now. Digital money was responsible for the easy banking process. With the help of digital money, people can access the services of a bank online with the comfort of being in their homes and not having the need to visit their bank physically. They can even make online money transfers with nothing but just their smartphones and an internet connection.

Nowadays, the most used payment modes are credit cards, debit cards, and e-wallets such as PayPal. Few these days prefer to carry cash to make a transaction. Banks and even economies face enormous consequences due to this evolution.

Traditionally, banks in the olden days would need a person to approach a branch of their bank in order to acquire the banking services provided by them. To operate this way, banks required a lot of money as they were required to pay their employees, maintain branches, etc. Because digital money came into existence, most banks have saved a lot on their operational costs as they would need lesser staff to carry out the activities. Moreover, they don't even have to operate many branches physically to improve their business.

However, when people physically approached banks to avail themselves of their services, banks could sell their products and services such as loans, financial planning services, insurance policies, wealth management services, etc. Now, it is quite hard for them as they would have to make a sale of these products and services online or by phone call. When it comes to an economy, the circulation of physical cash is immensely lowered with the use of digital money.

The most common type of digital money is the money that has been issued by a bank or a financial institution like a bank. Banks usually provide digital funds to their customers to use for trading, investing, or making payments. Banks are typically subject to some regulations, which require them to have a substantial amount of money within their physical location. There are no such regulations for digital money. Any bank can have digital money as much as they want without being subject to any regulations.

There is even availability of some banks that do not even have a physical presence. Even as they do not have any physical locations to serve their customers, they are known to handle billions and even trillions of monies without having any physical cash. Such banks are called online banks or digital banks. Nowadays, online banks are gaining a lot of popularity worldwide because of their offers and features provided to the customers. Online banks come up with exquisite offers as they can save a lot of money that brick-and-mortar banks spend to operate their physical branches. A few examples of such online banks are Revolut, Ally, Quontonic, Axos, Varo, etc.

As money is becoming rapidly digitalized these days, most people often do not understand digital money's working procedure. You might wonder, "How is anybody going to stop a person from producing their own digital money?". Yes, that is a valid question. There is a process that prevents people from double-spending digital money by creating their own money.

In the case of most financial institutions, this issue is addressed with the help of centralization. There will only be one particular authority that keeps track of all the financial data to who owns how much. People that make use of their digital money to make transactions online need to have an account. This account consists of a ledger containing all the data related to transactions made and balances maintained. Everyone trusts in the accuracy of the banks or other financial institutions for keeping track of this data, which is done with the help of their highly advanced computer systems. However, most of the alternative digital payment platforms' centralization has not been maintained effectively as accurately as it is done with the help of a blockchain.

**Advantages of digital money –** There are quite a handful of benefits when a person uses digital money.

One of the major benefits of using digital money is that you could make transactions with other people or businesses even when you are far away from them. To state an example for this, imagine if you are in the United States, and you want to send some money to a friend located in another country, let us say France. You could send the money over to them with the help of your mobile phone, in which you have an application of your bank's internet banking. You can also make the transfer if you have opted for your bank's phone banking feature. Simple as that.

When people make payments using their cards or e-wallets, they can have many benefits as well. Some of the significant benefits of making a payment with digital money are as follows:

- Saves time
- Efficient mode of payment
- Hassle-free
- Secure
- Easy to track

There are some other major benefits of using digital money, which we will discuss while we tell you about Bitcoin.

**Issues of Centralized Monetary System –** When a person or a particular group of people are given power over something, three main problems need to be addressed. These three issues are Corruption, Mismanagement, and

Control.

- Corruption:

Power and Corruption come hand-in-hand. Monetary authorities such as the Federal Reserve have all the necessary ability to create money and add value. Therefore, they have the power to control how value is created or relinquished within their respective economies. In such situations, these legal decrees allow success to unlimited financial power. If we take a look at an example for this, Wells Fargo ordered its employees to open a fake bank as well as fake credit card accounts. This was done to increase the company's profits, resulting in the company having a subsequent net worth for several years. Wells Fargo is not even a monetary authority. Hence, imagine what a monetary authority with full potential can do.

- Mismanagement:

Mismanagement is a scenario when the respective government acts against the benefits of the people living in that economy. Monetary authorities can allow financial institutions to introduce risky financial solutions that could be a significant threat to the economic structure. When a similar situation happened in the United States, and the country almost collapsed, the Federal Reserve decided against the public's benefits. It used up the money of the people, even when they were against this idea. Even though the Federal Reserve was able to save some of the major financial institutions from collapsing, it was still a measure taken regardless of the public interest.

Mismanagement can also be observed when a monetary authority prints an excessive amount of money without concentrating on the consequences. We are sure that you remember what happens when money gets printed excessively. An excellent example of this is Venezuela. Venezuelan government mismanaged the financial system and started to increase printing the money. By the end, money became so worthless that people began to weigh their money for acquiring goods and services.

- Control:

There is no need to say that a country's government would control all the money that people own. Because of the legal power that a specific government has, it can prevent people from using their money whenever it wants. The government can freeze people's accounts or prevent them from accessing their money lying within a bank. What will the government do if we have cash in hand, and will we be safe then? Well... the government can even make all the existing money useless by making them invaluable and creating new currency notes. The de-monetization situation in India would be considered an excellent example of this. When prime minister Modi came into power, he nullified the value of the existing currency notes of high value and started creating new ones instead. He even kept a limit for how much money can be withdrawn for a day so that people cannot deposit all the existing notes and get new ones instead. This method, even being burdensome for middle-class and poor people, lowered the excessive black money in India (as said by the Prime Minister of India).

# Chapter 7
# Precious Metals

Precious metals such as gold and silver also have a strong connection with money. To be more specific, they are not just a form of investment. Instead, they are considered money. Most of you might say that currencies such as the United States Dollar, British Pound, or European Euro are considered Money. Well, that is not true at all. You are talking about currencies, while we say that these precious metals are money (more of wealth).

So, why can't we use some other types of assets as money? Well, there are several reasons for that. To make money legit, it needs to qualify for specific characteristics. Let us now have a look at the traits that allow money to be legit.

- Durability:

Durability is one of the significant characteristics that allow money to have value. For example, we have discussed previously wheat or salt being used as a medium of exchange (money) in the olden days. Well, wheat or salt will not last long as precious metals like gold and silver do.

- Ability to be divided/separated:

Paintings or other forms are art are quite valuable, as a matter of fact. But you cannot use it to buy something of lower value or for several transactions. That is why divisibility is also an essential characteristic of making money legit.

- Convenience:

Take the aspect where we described more wheat that is needed to be taken to get more groceries, which has been discussed while talking about the evolution of money. Therefore, convenience is also essential.

- Consistency:

Assets such as real estate are often volatile when it comes to their prices. Assets should have a consistent value before they could be determined as a form of money.

- Intrinsic Value:

As for this aspect, even paper money isn't considered a legit type of money. A strip of paper used to create a $100 bill is not worth $100.

- Rarity:

The asset which would be considered as a true form of money would have to be rare. If it were available everywhere, everyone would have access to it, and it will not be much valuable. Iron, copper, or any other similar assets found abundantly cannot be used as money for this reason.

- Acceptability:

Almost every person should be familiar with the value of the asset that you determine as money. If only a few people are familiar with its value, they would only accept it to be used as money.

**Precious Metals are real money** – Therefore, the things that meet all the requirements mentioned are Precious Metals. Even financial assets or tangible assets will not be able to meet all the conditions mentioned above. Not only the value of metals like gold and silver has been maintained consistently. They have also seen a lot of growth in value over the years. Therefore, the purchasing power of precious metals will increase over time rather than losing all value. Suppose you consider all these facts and consider metals like gold and silver as a genuine and legit form of money. In that case, you will understand the fact that fiat money is not actually considered a valid form of money.

**Can the prices of precious metals be influenced** – To get an exact answer to this question, we might have to take a closer look at gold. Manipulation of gold prices means that anyone trying to gain authority over the prices of this metal. This happens in major financial markets, and there is no denying that. Gold traders try to influence the prices of gold with the help of financial instruments such as derivatives. By doing so, these traders can successfully create derivations from the actual value of the gold. However, this is only effective for a short period and will not be effective when considering over the long-term.

According to the Securities and Exchange Commission (SEC), manipulation is a deliberate act of tricking investors into making an investment. This can be done in many ways. Having artificial control over the market makes it look like there is a demand for a specific asset, or the markets will turn in the trader's favor when they invest in that asset. When talking precisely about gold, one method is most commonly seen and known as Price Suppression, which means manipulating gold prices to make it go downward.

Can anybody manipulate the price of gold or silver on a consistent basis?

When this question is asked, most people, who are gold traders and investors, would tell you that it can be manipulated. However, there are different views on this aspect. Most of them prove that there is actual manipulation with some good examples.

If you consider the long-term price histories of gold, you can see that most of them say it is absolutely false. To make it simpler for you to understand, precious metals' prices cannot be manipulated (at least not over a long-term).

As you have seen, we have checked all the intellectual characteristics considered as properties of ideal or real money. Most of the elements have been met by gold, which is the truest form of money. Comparing to gold, we cannot even consider fiat money as a real and ideal form of money. One of the best alternatives to fiat money, which has most of the ideal characteristics, is cryptocurrency. So, finally, let us find out what cryptocurrencies are and how they work.

# Chapter 8
# What is Bitcoin?

At last! We cover our main topic, gold among cryptocurrencies, one of the popular investment options available these days, none other than 'Bitcoin' – the primary cryptocurrency. From beginner-level investors to professional traders, Bitcoin has become one of the widely accepted modes of investment. However, some people might stay out of it due to its volatility, but it is similar to assets such as Gold for some others.

We have discussed everything in a detailed manner till now. Why shouldn't we do the same for Bitcoin? We will have an in-depth analysis of Bitcoin too. Bitcoin is a virtual currency invented in the year 2008 by a person/people known to the world by Satoshi Nakamoto. Not only us, but any other person in the world is unsure whether Satoshi Nakamoto is a single person or a group of people. We know for sure that this name is a pseudonym for the creator/creators of Bitcoin.

In January 2009, this Satoshi Nakamoto presented a whitepaper with a concept revolving around a peer-to-peer technology for decentralized virtual currency (cryptocurrency). A 'whitepaper'? No…! not some regular blank, white-colored paper. A whitepaper or white paper, in relevance to Bitcoin, is an informational document presented by a company or a non-profit organization. A white paper's main objective is to highlight the features and essential aspects of a product or service that the respective company will provide.

As it was created to be a cryptocurrency, Bitcoin presents a guarantee of minimal transaction fees when compared to other types of virtual payment mechanisms while maintaining its decentralized nature. It being a decentralized form of currency, no government or monetary authority shall have control over this currency; therefore, it comes with many advantages.

Bitcoin has become one of the popular forms of currency despite being a legal tender. Additionally, the invention of Bitcoin has led to the existence of many other forms of cryptocurrencies, some of which we have discussed earlier. Any other cryptocurrency other than Bitcoin itself is referred to as Altcoin. Usually, Bitcoin is abbreviated as BTC and is famous in that way since the beginning. But recently, International Standards Organization (ISO) started to use XBT instead of BTC. This ISO maintains a list of currencies that have been recognized worldwide. As Bitcoin is not associated with any of the countries in the world, the starting letter is kept as 'X' by the ISO. In this way, XBT was derived. Like Bitcoin, Gold is referred to as XAU by ISO, where X states that it is not an associated form of currency with any country, and AU refers to 'Aurum' (Latin name for Gold).

One Bitcoin has 1000 millibitcoins (mBTC) and 100,000,000 Santoshi's (sat). Until the end of 2020, the highest value that a Bitcoin could reach was approximately USD 29,000. By the time of writing this eBook, one bitcoin has a value of more than USD 58,000. This is a great improvement in the value when compared to the value of many other assets.

Once again, what is bitcoin? A cryptocurrency. Therefore, it is used for making a payment or transferring money. In order to be unique from other types of money, bitcoin does not rely on the monetary authorities such as central banks, which have full access and control towards the money supply. Not only that, but Bitcoin also offers the user the availability of making global online payments without having to pay any sort of additional fees. As the transactions are made with the help of a computer, the transaction will be done instantly.

Bitcoin is considered a fixed asset as there are only 21 million coins available in the world. Hence, when there would be an increase in the number of new investors, there would be a significant surge in its price since there is a limit on how many bitcoins can exist.

**Bitcoin address** – First of all, what exactly is a bitcoin address? For suppose let us imagine that you are sending a mail on your computer. When you send mail from your computer, you send that very particular mail with the help of a location known as an email address. This is considered the place from where you are sending the mail. Similarly, when you want to send a bitcoin to someone or receive a bitcoin from someone, you will need to have a location to do that. This location for doing so is virtual and is considered a bitcoin address. Usually, a bitcoin address contains a long series of letters as well as numbers.

People can either use their existing bitcoin address or change it every time a transaction takes place. However, security experts related to blockchain technology suggest changing your bitcoin address every time you send or receive a bitcoin. In this way, you can make up for your personal security as well as anonymity. Anonymity does not mean that you can just go ahead and make illegal transactions. It is suggested so that cybercriminals will not be able to trace your transactions.

Bitcoin addresses can range between 26 characters to 35 characters in length while containing alphabets and numbers. Usually, these bitcoin addresses begin with '1', '3', or 'bc1'. As of now, there are three bitcoin address formats in use.

1. P2PKH: starts with '1'
2. P2SH: starts with '3'
3. Bech32: starts with 'bc1'

**Bitcoin wallet** – Okay, we understood what a bitcoin address means. But earlier, we have said that you also would have to know what a bitcoin wallet means for having a better understanding. Yes! We are getting to that part. How can you or any other person generate a bitcoin address? You cannot just go ahead and type some letters and numbers on your computer and make it into a bitcoin address.

Therefore, for generating a bitcoin address, you will need a bitcoin wallet. A bitcoin wallet is a software that lets users send, receive or even store bitcoins on the respective blockchain network. To access your bitcoin wallet, you will be needing a private key, which will be provided to you during the time of creating your wallet. With the help of a bitcoin wallet, you can change your bitcoin address every time you make a payment or receive a payment.

**Types of wallets** – Usually, there are four types of bitcoin wallets, which we will discuss below.

- Mobile wallets:

Mobile wallets, as the name itself suggests, are wallets that can be accessed with the help of a smartphone. One key disadvantage of mobile wallets is that they can be accessed by people who can access your phone. Yes, it is true. The mobile wallet applications generally store the key on the app itself or on your phone to make it easy for you to access. Therefore, people who can open your phone might be able to send the funds to their account, and you can kiss them goodbye.

You can deal with this issue by opting for fingerprint authentication on your mobile for accessing your bitcoin wallet. However, if you are sleeping and the person can get your fingerprint without you even knowing it, you can kiss them goodbye again. Therefore, it is better to have a strong password for opening your mobile to have maximum security.

Bitcoin wallets can be downloaded and accessed with the Play Store (Android) or App Store (IOS). Even people with windows phones can download a bitcoin wallet. Given below are the best mobile bitcoin wallets for 2021.

- Bitcoin Wallet
- Edge (Aitbitz)
- Breadwallet
- Bither
- GreenBits
- Mycelium
- Green Address
- Coinomi
- Coinspace
- Electrum

- Web wallets:

Web wallets are bitcoin wallets that can be accessed with the help of using their website platform. Even web wallets have similar functionality to that of mobile wallets, along with the same types of risks involved.

Suppose a person close to you, such as an ex-girlfriend or friend who wants revenge or a close relative has gone rogue, intends to transfer your funds to their bitcoin wallet. In that case, they can do so by just having access to your computer and other details such as your mobile number, email address, and your birthday. By having access to these, they can switch the existing number to their phone as well.

You don't believe it? Let us have a look at how people do that on your computer. They can click on 'forgot password' for your email, and then you will get a text to change the password, which will be sent directly to the phone. After they successfully access your email, they can change the password to your Bitcoin wallet in a similar process. Voila! They can do whatever they want with the funds in your bitcoin wallet or even your bitcoin wallet as for that matter. It is highly recommended that you should tell your cell phone carrier to require a passcode before any changes can be made to your account details. In this way, you can make it highly impossible for the hackers to access (people who do not have access to your phone already).

Given below are the best web wallets (bitcoin wallets) for the year 2021:

- BitGo
- Blockchain
- BTC
- CoinBase
- CoinSpace
- Jaxx

- Desktop wallets:

Desktop wallets are just like mobile wallets. Mobile wallets are the applications that can be installed on a smartphone, and desktop wallets are the applications/software that can be installed on your computer. Compared to the security of web wallets and mobile wallets, desktop wallets are proven to be a bit better. However, there is no need to say that the advancement in technology is creating many opportunities for cybercriminals. Hackers are trying to find new ways to hack into these accounts as well.

While opting for a desktop wallet, it is better if you go for a wallet that encrypts your private key as well as your account recovery phrases. Given below are the best desktop wallets available in 2021.

- ArcBit
- Bitcore
- Bither
- Bitcoin ABC
- Bitcoin Core
- Bitcoin Unlimited
- Bitcoin XT
- Bitpie

- Copay
- Electron Cash
- Electrum
- Exodus
- Green Address
- Jaxx
- mSIGNA

• Hardware wallets:

Even most people who are familiar with bitcoins or using them might not be familiar with hardware wallets. Wait… Hardware wallets? Are they physical? But bitcoin is virtual, and how can it be stored in something that is physical? Hardware wallets are something similar to that of a hard drive for a computer. These hardware wallets can be plugged into your system for making transactions related to Bitcoin and then kept in a safe place afterward. As they won't be having continual access to the internet and can only be used when you want to use them, hardware wallets are the most efficient and secure way to store your bitcoins. you buy a hardware wallet on the internet, and the best hardware wallets available nowadays are given below:

- BitBox
- CoolWallet S
- KeepKey
- Ledger Nano S
- Trezor

• Paper wallet:

There is yet another method of storing bitcoins, which was prominently used between 2011 and 2016. This is an outdated and hazardous practice of storing bitcoins. A Paper Wallet, as you would typically imagine, is paper. This works by consisting of a private key and a bitcoin address, which are generated with the help of a website and then printed onto paper.

This method had many severe disadvantages such as difficulties related to printing, reuse of address, dangers involved with raw private keys, inefficient error correction, etc.

**Seed Phrase** – A seed phrase, which is also called a seed recovery phrase, or a backup seed phrase, or just seed, is a list of random words. This seed-phrase is used to recover the bitcoin funds. When creating a wallet, a seed will be generated, and the user would be asked to write it down on paper. Any person other than the owner who gets access to the seed phrase can steal the funds. Therefore, the seed phrase should be written on paper instead of typing into a website.

**Price History** – The price history of Bitcoin can be written as another book with at least 10,000 pages. There have been many fluctuations in the value of Bitcoin since it came into existence. These changes in the relevant price of Bitcoin were based on various factors such as the investor's interest, its guarantee of anonymity, people's satisfaction/dissatisfaction, etc.

The traditional banking sector became weak in people's minds after the financial collapse in 2008. This is one of the major reasons for cryptocurrencies to gain a lot of attention. Moreover, people started to believe in the concept of decentralization as it would be helpful for them if there was any situation such as the '2008 Financial Crisis' happens again.

Cryptocurrency markets have gained a lot of traction, and many investors and traders are attracted to Bitcoin and other cryptocurrencies as a good investment option. Nonetheless, it should be remembered that Bitcoin, like any other cryptocurrency, is a volatile asset, and the fluctuations in the price movements can be extremely advantageous or quite devastating. Regardless of the speculators' decisions for gaining profits based on the price momentum, there are many factors that influence Bitcoin.

The most significant changes took place from the year 2010. Given below is a step-by-step overview of the fluctuations in the price of Bitcoin since 2010.

- From January 2009 (when it was introduced) to March 2010, there were no exchanges or markets for Bitcoin. Usually, people who are cryptographic enthusiasts would send bitcoins to one another as a hobby.

In March 2010, a user named 'SmokeTooMuch' auctioned 10,000 bitcoins for just $50 and was not able to get buyers for that. Imagine what would have happened if you had bought those 10,000 bitcoins then? You would be sitting on a gigantic pile of money, which would be worth more than $564.4 million. Yes, we also wish for a time machine right now.

- In 2010, Bitcoin had the first-ever surge in its price when it increased from $0.0008 to $0.08.

- Later in 2011, the price of Bitcoin went from $1 to $32 by June. This is a 3200% gain over a period of just three months. However, it had a fall and reached $2 by November.

- In 2012, it had a slight improvement where the price was $4.80 at one point in May and reached $13.20 by 15th August.

- 2013 was one of the crucial years for Bitcoin as it had to face two significant fluctuations. At the beginning of the year 2013, the price of 1 Bitcoin was 13.40, but it had a considerable increase and reached $220 by April. Within a few days, the price went down to $70 by mid-April. Not just that, but in early October, the price was at $123.20. This went to a hefty $1,242 in November and $1,156.10 by December, and however, fell to $760 just three days after that.

- These fluctuations kept on happening, and the price of Bitcoin went from $850 to $580 in 2014. One of the primary reasons behind this is Mt. Gox, one of the earliest cryptocurrency exchanges globally.

How is a cryptocurrency exchange responsible for the price drop of a decentralized cryptocurrency? Well, the exchange filed for bankruptcy in 2014, and the reason was a cryptocurrency hack that took place in their exchange. During this hack, it was stated by the exchange that 850,000 bitcoins had been stolen from them.

- By the beginning of 2015, the price was approximately around $226, and by December, it reached an amount of $424.

- By January 2016, the price of Bitcoin was $378, and it reached $952 by the end of the year.

- 2017 was yet another major year while discussing the price movements of Bitcoin. While it was around $1,000 at the beginning of 2017, it had some falls and surges. But after it got to $975 on 25$^{th}$ March, it kept on having a significant increase in the price and reached $20,089 by December. This was considered the all-time highest for quite some time.

   This made Bitcoin gain a considerable reputation and a broad fan base among people all over the world. However, before the year came to an end, Bitcoin lost around one-third of its value within a short time span and stood at $14,000.

- By February 2018, this price fell by half and was less than $7000. By the end of 2018, the price went below $3,300, which is a 76% loss compared to its worth in the previous year. Naysayers, who do not suggest investing in cryptocurrencies, states this instance as an example.

- In the year 2019, the price started to rise gradually and reached around $12,000 by June. The price by the end of 2019 was about $7,250. This is considered a significant growth when compared to the price in the previous year.

- In January 2020, the price of bitcoin was around $9,545. After reaching $6,483 in March 2020, it reached more than $9,100 in June 2020. By December 2020, it was more than $28,000, which exceeded the previous all-time best.

- The highest in January 2021 was more than $39,000 on 14$^{th}$ January 2021, and as of February 2021, the highest is $58,200 on 21$^{st}$ February.

*Note: All the values mentioned above are just to provide an estimation of the price movements of Bitcoin during that respective period. Some of the values might have been lower/higher than the actual values. However, the difference between the actual values and the real values will not differ by much. There might be a very slight difference; if not, the values might be accurate.*

Based on the overall fluctuation in the price movement of Bitcoin so far, we can come to an understanding that the value will be substantially higher given the required amount of time. Based on the analysis of the early stages of Bitcoin's price movement, the value depended on the use of Bitcoin as a currency and its trading activity. However, the traditional mode of transactions did not lose their touch, and most of the cryptocurrencies were never used as a daily mode of payment. This is mainly because people see the actual nature of bitcoin. Instead of using it for payments, they opt to buy and hold it for a specific period of time to preserve their money. In the old days, people made use of gold in this process.

**Other forms of Bitcoin–** yes, most of us know bitcoin and hear about it every now and then. However, some of you might have even heard some other terms, such as Bitcoin Cash (BCH) and Bitcoin Gold (BTG). What are these?

Bitcoin Cash was created to lower the transaction time, which is one of the most popular issues faced by Bitcoin. In the beginning, Bitcoin was launched with a 1MB block for the reduction of spam and fraud. As the days passed, the transactions started to take a lot of time to happen, which is very depressing. This 1MB block started having many difficulties because of its small size and needed an efficient resolution. That is when Bitcoin Cash was created, with an 8MB block. This helps in the block creation process and transaction time by speeding the process. Bitcoin Cash, just like Bitcoin, is available on many of the existing cryptocurrency exchanges.

On the other hand, another issue that was being faced by the miners was related to the necessary equipment. To mine a bitcoin, they would require a lot of equipment that would cost them a lot of money. This would also take up a lot of energy as well, for running the equipment such as GPUs, ASICs, and as well as other things such as cooling fans.

To avoid this issue and make it simple so that even ordinary people could be able to mine bitcoin, Bitcoin Gold was created. With Bitcoin Gold's help, people could start mining Bitcoin, just like they used to do for Bitcoin in the beginning. For this, they will not even be needing advanced equipment anymore; only a regular computer would suffice.

# Chapter 9
# What is Cryptocurrency?

To gain an understanding of this concept using the fundamental terms, we see two different words in the term Cryptocurrency. The first word that we can observe is Crypto, and the second one is Currency. We have covered a lot of information about Currency and how it works. Therefore, there is no way that you might not know what that means. The first word, however, is Crypto. So, what is Crypto? The usual meaning that crypto refers to would be something like secret or hidden. However, the word Crypto is referring to the phrase Cryptography.

**Cryptography** – Cryptography is a process, which is used to hide some information or data in order to keep it a secret. This process is carried out by creating codes that make the information invisible. So, if it is hidden, then what exactly is the purpose of having it all? Well, by making it invisible, it does not erase or delete that specific information. Instead of that, it actually makes the data invisible to the people who aren't authorized to have access to that particular information. Therefore, the data secured with the help of cryptography is only intended to be readable by the people or users who have the actual authorization to access that data. In simple words, we can say that cryptography allows a secret to maintain its secrecy.

In the Information Security field, cryptography is used on various levels. The information that has been encrypted using the method cryptography cannot be decrypted unless the person who wants to access that data has a specific key that can decode it. In other contexts, cryptography might also be called Cryptology. Some of the common algorithms used in the process of cryptography are as follows:

- Secret Key Cryptography (SKC):

The term 'Secret' is used in the name itself, which leaves us with no need to explain it in a detailed manner. To put it simply, this type of algorithm uses only one key, which is for both encryptions and decryptions. This makes it one of the highly secure algorithms while encrypting data.

- Public Key Cryptography (PKC):

Wait… Public? Well, we said that cryptography is supposed to keep our data or information private. Why is an algorithm named 'Public' used in such a process? Do not worry. This type of algorithm makes use of two keys, namely a Public Key and a Private key. The Public key is accessible by anyone, whereas a private key is only accessible by a specific individual. A little bit confusing, right? Well, let us see a small example to understand this.

Suppose if you are sending some data and intend it to be read by a specific person. So, when you send that data, it is received by a particular person instead of somebody else. Here, you can make use of PKC, where you encrypt the data using your public key, and then it can only be accessed by the person who has the private key. Back on track? Great!!! Let's go ahead.

- Hash Functions:

Hash Functions are very different from PKC and SKC. These do not have a key, and for that reason, they are named One-way Encryption. Hash Functions are applied to encrypt the data that needs to remain unchanged.

**Cryptocurrency** – Having understood cryptography, you can now be able to easily understand what a cryptocurrency means. A cryptocurrency is nothing but a digital currency or virtual currency, which has been secured with the help of cryptography. As cryptocurrencies are secured using cryptography, there is no chance that people can counterfeit this currency or double-spend it. Almost all cryptocurrencies are decentralized forms of money and operate based on blockchain technology. But we have not discussed what a 'Blockchain' is? Yes, you are right. So, let's have a peek into the details of blockchain.

**Blockchain** –Blockchain, although the term might look rather complex, it is not that complex. Blockchain is a database. So, what is a database? The database is a bundle of information that has been stored in an electronic format, which means it is present on a computer or any other similar system that can store data. Usually, the information that is present within a database is present in a highly organized manner. This makes it easy to search or filter the data when we need to find specific information. And by a database, we do not mean something such as a spreadsheet. We suggest something far more complex, large, and is used to store significantly vast amounts of data. By storing data in a database, it can easily be accessed by more than a few people to find information easily as well as quickly.

Databases that substantially large might have electronic devices that might be able to contain such vast amounts of data. In such cases, massive databases are stored on servers, which are made with the help of enormously powerful computers. In certain instances, these servers would be required to be built by using thousands of computers in order to effectively maintain all the operations and manage the storage capacity. Then only, these servers will stay efficient and can be accessed by many users at a time. Similar to something such as a spreadsheet, specific businesses create databases. They are managed by the people who have total control over the database's operations and the data lying within it.

So, a database is what a blockchain is. Well, not exactly. The significant difference between a general database and a blockchain is the structuring of the actual data. In blockchains, all the data is maintained within small bundles of information, which are generally called Blocks. These blocks have limits for the actual size that can be stored within them. When a block gets completely filled with data, it is connected/chained to another block that has been filled entirely. This formation of a chain by connecting all the blocks that contain the data is known as Blockchain.

The database is a tad bit different as it fills data into tables, unlike the blockchain that chains several blocks of information together. Henceforth, all the blockchains are databases, while not all the databases are considered blockchains. Not only that, but the blockchain system also keeps track of the timeline of data that cannot be reversed when it is stored with a decentralized nature. After a bock gets filled completely, it is set up in stone and made part of this data timeline. An exact timestamp is given to each specific block in a blockchain when it gets added into the chain.

These blockchains are considered publicly accessible ledgers that allow the users to record their transactions, control them, and make changes to those. Let us compare it to something like Wikipedia, for example. Anyone can create content on Wikipedia, and like that, the total power doesn't just reside within a single person.

We must, however, consider some aspects before thinking that everything of blockchain will be similar to something such as Wikipedia. For example, Wikipedia users are first offered permission to make changes to the content, among all which are located on an integrated server. Therefore, every time users enter Wikipedia, and they are provided with an updated version of the actual page. Adding to that, the regulation of all the existing data resides within the administrators. These administrators are offered all the required permissions and access via the main authority at the actual center. Therefore, Wikipedia and its operational procedure are most likely to be like databases of centralized institutions such as banks, insurance companies, etc.

In the case of blockchain, it is quite different as the updates to the information are done independently. Each and every change that is made within the system is done on a master copy and can be seen by all the users.

How does a blockchain actually work in reality? To answer that, we will have a close look at the step-by-step procedure of blockchains and how cryptocurrency transaction history is stored.

- First, when a person makes a transaction, that information related to the transaction is entered.

- The transaction details are then transmitted to a network of peer-to-peer computers that are located all over the world.

- The network of computers will solve equations using the required methods so that it can be able to confirm whether a transaction is valid or not.

- After the validity of the transactions has been verified and it has been confirmed that they are legit, they are bundled into blocks.

- These blocks are chained to each other after the block gets filled with data. This is helpful in creating the history of transactions, which is quite large and permanent as well.

- Finally… Voila! The transaction is complete.

Finally, in this way, blockchains are useful for the transaction of most cryptocurrencies. The principal purpose of a cryptocurrency is to create a decentralized form of money without requiring the involvement of banks, governments, or any other centralized monetary authorities.

**Nodes -** We already said that blockchain stores all the required data in the form of blocks, and these blocks of data are stored on things called Nodes, which can be understood as small servers. Nodes can be typical laptops or computers or even gigantic servers, which are responsible for the formation of the infrastructure of a blockchain.

All the nodes on a blockchain are interlinked with each other. Every time something is entered within a node, this data would be transferred to other nodes as well. By doing so, all the nodes will be able to stay updated with accurate information. Finding it hard? Let us see an example in general terminology so that you can get an exact idea of what a node means.

Let us assume there are three chat groups on three different computers. Now, when a message is sent in the chat group using one computer, it gets updated within the other two computers, which are the chat group members. Now, think of the chat groups in each computer as a specific node and the message as the blockchain data's history. Thank us later!

So, what exactly do these nodes do, or what is the specific operational procedure? Well, let us see. When a miner enters a new block of transaction history into the blockchain, the data is sent over to all the nodes present within a network. Depending on the data's validity (signature and transactions), nodes accept or reject that block. If the node accepts the new block (meaning the data is legitimate), it is stored on top of the data blocks that are already being stored.

To make it even easier to understand, nodes check whether the data is valid or not. If the data on the block is not valid, the nodes reject it. If the data of the new block is valid, the block gets saved and stored. Now, this block of data is sent over to other nodes, which updates the transaction history to all other nodes as well.

**Blockchain Mining** – Blockchain Mining is the process used by people (called miners) to secure the data within a blockchain and verify it. Miners add the transaction history data to the worldwide public ledger of the past transactions. Yes, we understand that all this might be a tad bit difficult to understand if you are a beginner. So, let us have a look at the details in a simplified manner.

- When a transaction takes place in a blockchain, the information must be recorded and put inside a block. As we know, the block needs security and encryption.

- Who does that? This is where the blockchain miners come to the rescue. The miners are considered as the contributing members of the blockchain network.

- In order to encrypt the information, miners are required to solve a cryptographic puzzle, which involves a trial-and-error method, or it would be more accurate to call it a guess-and-check method.

- By following this method, the miners must find the appropriate cryptographic hash solution for the block.

- Usually, this process requires a lot of efficient and reliable hardware (with specific applications). By having such a piece of tech in their hands, a person can be the first to crack a puzzle and then verify and secure the block.

- When a miner secures a block, the block is added to the blockchain and verified by the nodes existing within that blockchain. This process of verification by other nodes is called consensus (which means agreement) and happens with the help of algorithms called consensus algorithms.

- By doing so, a miner is rewarded with a coin that has been newly created. When a miner gets rewarded for this type of work, the process of the consensus algorithm used in the process would be referred to as Proof of Work.

We will have a more focused look at mining and miners when we talk about Bitcoin.

**Miners and Nodes –** A miner must run a full node to make sure that the new block contains valid data. When the miner might not be able to run a full node, it cannot be determined whether all the transactions in blockchain transaction history are valid or not. On the other hand, nodes can also be received, stored, and their transaction history can be broadcasted with the help of just a device, like a server. These devices might not be able to create new blocks of transaction history on their own. For that, a miner's involvement is definitely necessary.

**Nodes securing the blockchain** – Nodes are considered to be of two types, which are online nodes and offline nodes. Online nodes are the operational nodes that constantly receive, save, and send all the updated information to other nodes. This is not the case when it comes to offline nodes. An offline node would have to refresh and update all the existing transaction history within the online nodes. For this, an offline node that comes back online would have to download all the blocks that have been added to the respective blockchain after that specific node went offline. This process of getting updated with the existing transaction history in the blockchain is called Synchronizing with the blockchain.

All the data existing within a blockchain can be run on a single node. Anyhow, when a single node has all the data, it becomes vulnerable to some issues such as hacking, power outage, or a crash. It is better to have many nodes working so that all these issues can be dealt with. When blockchain data is spread among various devices globally, the chances of the data getting lost are less likely—the more, the merrier.

In unfortunate events such as all the systems becoming inaccessible due to something, one node will be enough to keep the blockchain working. If all the nodes go offline, then the node with all the blockchain data would be sufficient to make the data accessible again. The transactions that occur when all the nodes go offline cannot be restored again, no matter what you do.

**Running a node** – In the case of most of the blockchains, thousands of online nodes exist. Any individual who can get their hands on the transaction history of a blockchain can run a node by downloading that specific transaction history. People who want to see a world full of people making use of cryptocurrencies run nodes voluntarily. They might even form a community related to this and take care of all the activities related to blockchain technology, such as development, security, etc. In some cases, people might do it out of a hobby or just for fun.

Running a node does not require a vast amount of knowledge and experience.

Instead, people who are familiar with technology and how it works might be able to perform the task accurately. There is not even a necessity of highly advanced equipment as well. However, some specific blockchains have a lot of data that needs to be stored and require devices with a vast amount of storage space for running a full node-people who just want to make use of mobile or web applications called wallets. With these wallets' help, the transaction history is broadcasted to the entire blockchain without having the user required to download all the data on their own devices.

**Masternodes** – Masternodes are used in some blockchains, which are more robust when compared to the traditional nodes. Apart from validating, saving, and broadcasting the transaction history, masternodes are responsible for some other activities as well. For example, Masternodes facilitate events related to the blockchain, such as managing voting events, executing protocol operations, enforcing the rules and regulations of that specific blockchain technology, and others. Unlike normal nodes, masternodes are online all the time and house gigantic storage space. A masternode can be considered as a substantial server that is present on the network. As maintaining a masternode requires a lot of equipment, electricity, storage space, up-time, etc., payments are provided in the form of interest for doing so.

Masternodes cannot be run by an average individual as there are chances that a person might misuse the power of control. Therefore, people who want to host a masternode must pay a hefty amount of money in the form of cryptocurrency as collateral. When the blockchain rules are not followed by the host or the host misuses the power of masternodes, this collateral would be taken away. The interest received by the host is entirely dependent on the deposit made by them as collateral.

One of the most famous blockchains that use a masternode feature is Dash (DASH). The minimum amount required to qualify for hosting a Dash's masternode would be needed to pay 1,000 DASH. By the time of writing this book, one Dash is at the north of $164. Just taking $160 into consideration, a person would be required to pay $160,000 for hosting a masternode of Dash. However, the interest rate can be quite attractive as the interest rate would be considered a handsome return. As per the details presented within the Dash website, 45% of the block reward is offered to the miner when a new block is discovered. Then 45% is offered to the people who host masternodes, and 10% is kept for maintaining the budget system.

**Consensus Algorithms –** Consensus Algorithms ensure that every block added to that network is true and is agreed by all the nodes present within a distributed or decentralized computing network.

As discussed before, blockchains are decentralized networks, which target on providing permanence and security to the data. Without having any sort of involvement from the central government or any other monetary authority, transactions within a blockchain technology are highly enriched with security and are valid.

There are transactions worth millions (if not billions) that are carried within each and every blockchain all over the world. Because of the vast number of transactions that are being carried out in reality, the process can get quite complex. If the blockchain is not able to acquire consensus, events such as double-spending attacks can happen.

In general terminology, a consensus algorithm is an algorithm related to computer science required to ensure that all the distributed processes or devices agree on a single data value. With the help of a consensus algorithm, all the nodes on a blockchain come to an agreement when it comes to validating the data in a block. In this way, blockchain maintains the integrity and security within its operations with consensus algorithms' help. Let us have a look at some of the most popularly used consensus algorithms in the world currently.

- Proof of Work (PoW):

Proof of Work's actual concept was first introduced in 1993 by Cynthia Dwork and Moni Naor. It is a process of creating a cryptographic hash. This concept came into the light again when Satoshi Nakamoto created a whitepaper for Bitcoin in 2008.

This is a commonly used way of confirming the validity of the transactions. The primary objective is that the people (miners) who confirm a transaction must undergo a process of solving a cryptographic puzzle with this algorithm's help. The result produced from this would become easy to be understandable.

The first person to run a complete node by doing all the necessary calculations will receive a reward from the blockchain network. Even though many nodes compete against each other in this process, the first node to crack the puzzle gets the reward.

This process involves a vast of money regarding the energy required to run the equipment, such as specialized computers called ASICs (Application-Specific Integrated Circuit). Only one node gets the reward, which is the first node to complete the cryptographic hash puzzle.

- Proof of Stake (PoS):

This is also one of the most widely used consensus algorithms in blockchain networks. With this algorithm's help, a node with a vast number of resources (cryptocurrency coins or tokens) is chosen for generating the next block in the specific blockchain. In the PoW algorithm, the reward is presented to the node that solves the cryptographic hash functions. Whereas in the PoS algorithm, the reward is presented to the node that executes the transaction.

The node that can be chosen for executing the transaction can be random among the nodes with abundant resources or random among the nodes that have been there for quite some time.

There is no need for highly specialized equipment or a substantial amount of energy like in the PoW. To house a double-spending attack, the attacker would be required to possess more than 50% of the entire cryptocurrency (related to that blockchain) that exists. This is impossible. However, as the resources have to be plenty, there can be consequences that can lead to centralization.

Some other consensus algorithms include Delegated Proof of Stake (DPoS), Leased Proof of Stake (LPoS), Proof of Capacity (PoC), Proof of Importance (PoI), Proof of Activity (PoA), etc. However, we will mainly be seeing about the Proof of Work and Proof of Stake, and hence, there is not a necessity to know about all these consensus algorithms.

**Pros and Cons** – we will now have a brief look at some of the significant advantages as well as disadvantages of blockchain.

First of all, let us see what the advantages are that we can get by using blockchain.

- Enhanced accuracy in the process of verification by removing human involvement.

- There is no necessity for a third-party verification process, which means the additional costs of third-party interference can be avoided.

- Because blockchains are decentralized, which means nobody can mess with the process to gain profits.

- Transactions made with the help of a blockchain are secure, effective, and private.

- Serves as the best alternative to the banks, especially in the regions where people are not satisfied with their monetary authorities.

Now, having discussed the advantages of blockchain, let us see what the disadvantages are.

- When it comes to mining in blockchain technology, a considerable amount of money is required.

- Time taken for the transactions might be a bit slow for some blockchains.

- They are majorly used for illegal activities such as tax evasion and money laundering.

- Regulations like no refund or no-cancellation policy, which are rather inconvenient for most people.

**ICO** – ICO (Initial Coin Offering) is for cryptocurrencies, similar to what IPO (Initial Public Offering) is for stocks and companies. The ICO is a new coin that a company has created as a way of raising money. People who invest in ICOs are offered a crypto token, which the company issues. This cryptocurrency token can be utilized for making use of the services provided by that company. If it cannot be used in that way, it will then represent a stake in the company or the project that launched ICO.

Throughout history, many ICOs were proven to be successful and gained many profits to the investors. Some other ICOs were fraud or performed poorly while resulting in a loss for the investors.

To purchase an ICO, people would require a minimum level of knowledge on how to make use of cryptocurrency wallets and cryptocurrency exchanges. As ICOs are mostly unregulated, investors must proceed with an extreme level of caution before making an investment in them.

**Comparison of Cryptocurrencies with fiat money and gold** - In most cases, cryptocurrencies have a terrible reputation because of the purposes they might be used for, the high volatility, vulnerability of the structure, etc. However, there have been many advantages of cryptocurrencies, such as divisibility, transparency, etc.

We have spent a lot of time knowing about gold, fiat currencies, and all. We have also discussed that cryptocurrencies are the nearest for money that satisfies all the requirements for a type of money to be considered ideal or real money. So, how exactly are cryptocurrencies better than fiat currencies? Well, we will see that now.

- Low risk of disruption:

As cryptocurrencies are not under the power of a specific individual or a particular country, there is no supreme power that can interfere with cryptocurrencies' operational procedure. David John Grundy, who happens to be the global blockchain head at Danske Bank, stated that the only possible way a person might be able to shut down the system of blockchain is by shutting the internet down. Every reader might be familiar with the fact that the internet is not going anywhere anytime soon. Therefore, technically, it is not at all possible for blockchain technology to cease to exist. This leads us to our statement that cryptocurrencies have a low risk of disruption when compared to some other forms of money.

- Portability:

Keeping the digital money aside, traditional fiat money is usually difficult (not that hard, but yet hard) to transfer if the transactions involved vast sums of money. Therefore, cryptocurrencies, being virtual money, have the required portability feature. The transfers of a cryptocurrency can be made using electronic devices such as smartphones, computers, etc. By just having a good internet connection and a smartphone, you can transfer money whenever you want and wherever you want.

- Appreciation while storing:

An asset would be considered as an ideal form of money only when its value does not decrease over time. This feature will come in handy when the asset is being stored. If a person holds a specific cryptocurrency (as a form of investment) and the value of that particular cryptocurrency cannot increase over time or experiences a decrease in its value, it would be rather dissatisfactory to the person who is storing that specific cryptocurrency. Even though there have been many fluctuations in the value of cryptocurrencies such as Bitcoin, the value has increased when stored for an extended period of time. An asset's ability to maintain its value and not be decreased over time is estimated based on that asset's quantitative and qualitative analysis.

Because cryptocurrencies can maintain their value when stored, people often invest in cryptocurrencies or hold them for a specific period of time. However, the reliability cannot be determined to be exact as cryptocurrencies are highly volatile in nature.

We compare cryptocurrencies with the proper ideal form of money, i.e., precious metals such as gold and silver. When more people start trusting cryptocurrencies, which they will do eventually, these assets' value will experience a hike and help maintain the value when stored—not just keeping the value. Instead, the value will see an increase given the required amount of time.

- Deflationary:

Just like precious metals that exist in limited quantities and cannot be created in excess when needed, cryptocurrencies exist in certain amounts as per the protocols. We already know that when money gets printed excessively, it will cause inflation in the specific country. Unlike fiat money that can be printed excessively as per the government's wish, cryptocurrencies must exist in limited quantities. For instance, Bitcoin has a cap of 21 million units per the blockchain protocols and cannot exist more than that. Similarly, Litecoin has a limit of 84 million units per the operational protocols and cannot be created more than that. This feature of cryptocurrencies makes them free from inflation or deflationary.

We also discussed how supply and demand work within a country, how an increase in supply or an increase in demand will affect the country. Keeping that in mind, soon, there will be an increase in the value of cryptocurrencies. Why? We have a strong reason to believe so. When a particular currency is limited, its quantity gradually decreases over time as it gets used up to purchase goods and services. When something becomes rare, the value of that particular asset will increase over time, whether for precious metals or cryptocurrencies. Therefore, we can anticipate an increase in cryptocurrencies' purchasing power, especially over the long term.

- Independent:

Cryptocurrencies are not connected to other asset classes in any way possible. Assets such as fiat money or stocks can fluctuate depending on the government's decisions or any other centralized monetary authority. Precious Metals also share this very same unique feature and are not linked/connected to any other assets. The value of precious metals or cryptocurrencies stays independent and can withstand the major financial decisions or policy changes that occur within a specific country. Therefore, cryptocurrencies or precious metals cannot be tampered with by monetary authorities or financial institutions, making them have a reduced amount of risk of losing the value or being influenced.

- Intrinsic Value:

Assets that are the best for storing while maintaining their value happen to have underlying properties that serve the purpose of maintaining that value. In order to describe it in a simple way for you, an asset can ideally preserve its value when it has a specific use. Take gold as an example. Gold is used for making jewelry or creating electronic parts such as semiconductors (which most people might not be familiar with). Hence, gold can maintain its value and has an intrinsic utility value. Similarly, real estate is used to build houses, apartments, or any other sort of infrastructure. The value of real estate property is determined by factors such as how many structures can be built, access to services, etc.

Just like gold and real estate, cryptocurrencies also have sound potential. To be specific, cryptocurrency is the most advanced method available, which would change the world's entire financial transaction process in the near future. Most of the fields that would make use of the applications of cryptocurrencies are the fields related to financial transactions made online such as contracts, payments, records keeping, and many more. Additionally, cryptocurrencies such as Bitcoin, Litecoin, Ethereum, etc., are being popularly accepted worldwide. This is another contributing factor that leads to an increase in these cryptocurrencies' value over the long term.

- Cannot create fake cryptocurrencies:

Blockchain technology is considered one-of-a-kind when it comes to clearing the way for online transactions, data maintenance, etc. Because of this, nobody can create counterfeit variants of cryptocurrencies. As the technology gets more and more advanced, there will not be any possibility for people to create fake cryptocurrencies and use them as actual cryptocurrencies.

- Cannot be manipulated:

Cryptocurrencies have market capitalizations worth billions of dollars, especially when it comes to particular cryptocurrencies such as Bitcoin and Ether. To manipulate the value of such currencies, one must have a lumpsum amount of money for buying enough units. If a person cannot buy enough units of a specific cryptocurrency, he/she cannot be able to manipulate its price. For example, Bitcoin has a market capitalization of nearly $647 billion as of recent stats. To manipulate the prices by altering the demand and supply, one would need to buy at least $150 billion worth of Bitcoin. The same applies to other cryptocurrencies such as Ethereum, Tether, etc.

- Anybody can participate:

When we look at stocks or other investment vehicles, people need to have a considerable amount of money to make an investment or at least a substantial amount of money. However, the entry is set to low compared to those amounts when it comes to cryptocurrencies. People who want to invest money that is considered a small amount to invest can also participate. Considering this factor, many investors are involved with making an investment in cryptocurrencies, which makes it even harder to manipulate the prices for one specific individual's profit.

- Secure:

In general, cryptocurrencies are recorded in a blockchain. This blockchain technology and a constant review of the system by the users make it highly impossible for a person to hack cryptocurrencies. However, if a person gets access to your cryptocurrency wallet, then you can kiss it goodbye. It has been reported that approximately 980,000 bitcoins were stolen from cryptocurrency exchanges by the end of 2017.

# <u>Chapter 10</u>
# More about Cryptocurrencies:

**History -** As for the history of cryptocurrencies, the starting period dates to the 1990s. During that time, an American cryptographer called David Chaum invented the first-ever online money in the Netherlands, named DigiCash. DigiCash was encrypted with the help of a famous algorithm during that time known as 'RSA' (Rivest-Shamir-Adleman). This method is also being used nowadays and is a type of public-key cryptography algorithms. This eCash product, along with the technology created by David, got a lot of attention from the media. Even Microsoft became interested in acquiring DigiCash for a sum of $180 million to provide this in their Windows OS. But the offer was rejected for some particular reasons. Because of these huge mistakes, the company went bankrupt in the year 1998.

The next set of companies came up with some effective changes made to the alternate payment systems and the operational procedures. Among these second-generation companies, PayPal was considered an absolute winner because of its efficiency and accessibility. The main reason behind the success of PayPal is its ability to offer peer-to-peer transactions, especially between individuals and merchants. PayPal became so popular that people started to prefer PayPal as an alternate payment option if they did not opt for card payment.

There was even a company that became famous during the same period as PayPal. However, this company did not actually provide services related to online money. Instead, it offered online gold services. Online Gold? Is that even possible? Well, as a matter of fact, it is, and the company's name is e-Gold. This company allowed the customers to deposit actual gold and provided them with credits known as e-Gold or gold credits. E-Gold operated efficiently for a specific period until there was a time when scams and frauds such as the Ponzi scheme came to light. After such illegal activities came into existence, e-Gold was closed.

After the mortgage crisis took place in 2008, most of the world's leading financial institutions were affected. Considering this as a warning bell, people started to search for something more effective, and then blockchain and cryptocurrencies happened. And later in the year 2009, a person called Satoshi Nakamoto created Bitcoin, which will discuss in a while.

**Advantages** – There are some advantageous features while making use of cryptocurrencies.

- Firstly, we can see that online money's main feature is to make the transaction process easy and effective. With the help of online money such as cryptocurrencies, people can make transfers regardless of the distance between the sender and the recipient.

- Adding to that, banks, and credit card companies, which are a third party in the transfer process, can be avoided when opted for cryptocurrencies. Usually, banks and other financial institutions use a lot of technology to make sure that the payment process is secure. However, this process is different when it comes to cryptocurrencies. While making a transfer using cryptocurrencies, the transaction process is secured with the help of algorithms such as Public Keys, Private Keys, etc. There are some other forms of incentive systems involved in this process as well, such as Proof of Work or Proof of Stake.

- The cryptocurrencies are usually held within a crypto wallet which has a public key and a private key, where the private key is known only to the owner who is required to sign the transactions, making them secure.

- The transfers of funds are completed by charging exceptionally low fees, allowing the users to get rid of substantial transaction costs applicable when money is transferred with the help of banks or other financial institutions. We have discussed some of the major advantages of using cryptocurrencies earlier, such as Portability, Low Risk of Disruption, etc. We were comparing cryptocurrencies with assets such as fiat money and gold.

- Inflation. Yes, we have discussed that inflation could be controlled when we make use of cryptocurrencies. This is due to two main reasons, namely, decentralization and limited quantity. Every cryptocurrency was launched with a specific limit during the time of its launch. Therefore, when the demand for these increases, there would be a significant increase in the value as well. This would be a handy feature to cope with the inflation that might take place. And as cryptocurrencies are decentralized, no specific person has authority over them. There will not be any possible cases where a person or an authority would print more of them to deal with the financial consequences or gain profits. Therefore, we consider cryptocurrencies to be the best way to deal with inflation, or we can just call them "Inflation-proof'.

- No specific monetary authority looks after the development of cryptocurrencies, and therefore, there will not be any involvement from any centralized authority or the government. The developmental activities are done by miners/developers, and they are paid with the transaction fees for doing so. Hence, the actions of cryptocurrencies are considered to be self-governed.

- Cryptocurrency can be purchased with many fiat currencies such as the US Dollar, European Euro, British Pound, Japanese Yen, and many more. By using cryptocurrency wallets and cryptocurrency exchanges, people can be able to convert and trade one cryptocurrency with another and make profits from it. They are charged with minimal transaction fees for doing all these activities related to cryptocurrency trading.

**Disadvantages** – Having known everything about the advantages of cryptocurrencies, let us now look at some of the disadvantages associated with cryptocurrencies.

- The most significant disadvantage of using cryptocurrencies is also considered an advantageous one. However, it is not advantageous to the general public, but it is beneficial for conducting illegal activities like tax evasion, money laundering, etc. The specific anonymous nature of a cryptocurrency is responsible for carrying out such types of unlawful activities. However, people who boast about cryptocurrencies' useful nature state that this anonymous nature is considered a protection from the repressive government (for people such as activists). However, not all cryptocurrencies have an anonymous nature, as some among them do.

- So, we can launder money and evade taxes using cryptocurrencies? Well, not really. Bitcoin has played a very active role in helping the authorities trace out and arrest many criminals using its forensic analysis. There might be the availability of one or two cryptocurrencies that might help aid with the above-mentioned illegal activities. However, we highly recommend that you use the technology for the right purposes and not try to get involved in such types of activities.

- If there were ever to occur any data loss or malfunction of the technology, it would mean that people would have to lose their money as well. Even though most people claim that it is highly unlikely for such an event to occur, there is a possibility of it happening.

- The developers of this technology make continuous efforts to create robust untraceable code, excellent defensive mechanisms against hackers, impenetrable security protocols, and more. This is a relief. But you must remember while if you were ever to lose your private key, which is used to access the wallet, then it is time to bid farewell to your money—locked away forever. Therefore, technical issues will result in loss of money in any event, such as malfunction or loss of the key.

- You should also consider that the evolution of technology and advancement of security tools has its negative effects. Yeah, it is about hackers. People (a handful) are becoming very advanced with their hacking skills that they are even hacking official government websites, defense websites, renowned financial institutions, and many more.

Compared to those, what exactly would be the technology used for cryptocurrency. Advanced hackers can steal money existing within people's wallets, and we have seen many such cases happen before. Most of the cryptocurrency exchanges and wallets are becoming secure as the security is getting advanced, yet we should always take a look at the other side of the coin (negative impacts).

- We have learned that cryptocurrencies are decentralized, and no single person has the authority over the value of the cryptocurrency. But to what extent? Cryptocurrencies are still managed and controlled by organizations that created them or those who belong to those very organizations. There is a chance that these creators or organizations can manipulate the value and make some large fluctuations take place in the respective cryptocurrencies' value. Even major cryptocurrencies such as Bitcoin itself are prone to these types of fluctuations caused by manipulations. We can see the value of Bitcoin in the year 2017, for example, when the value doubled more than once.

- In certain specific cases, people who want to trade with cryptocurrencies cannot find a suitable fiat currency. This is because some types of cryptocurrencies might not be available to be traded using more than a handful of fiat currencies. Therefore, people might be required to transfer the money into some other type of cryptocurrency and then exchange it to their desired cryptocurrency. This process would generally involve additional transaction fees while resulting in unnecessary costs.

- Finally, another extremely significant disadvantage of using cryptocurrencies is the no refund and no cancellation policy. If there were ever to occur any issue between the two parties that transact money with the help of cryptocurrencies, there would not be a possibility for the sender to get his/her money back. As harsh it might sound, it is the bitter truth of cryptocurrencies.

- Moreover, if you accidentally send a digit extra or send it to the wrong person, then the money that has been transferred would most likely be lost. Many people, who are scammers, try to sell goods in cryptocurrencies. In that way, people would end up paying money for the goods or services that they did not receive or won't receive.

**Major types of Cryptocurrencies** – As our main topic revolves around Bitcoin, we will get it to it in the end. Meanwhile, let us have a look at some of the other major cryptocurrencies in the world. We cannot cover all the cryptocurrencies in the world. Hence, we will only have a look at some of the major cryptocurrencies in the world, which are familiar to most of you.

- Ethereum (ETH):

Ethereum (ETH) is a major cryptocurrency, which is almost as popular as Bitcoin. It is a decentralized software platform that helps in Decentralized Applications (dApps) and Smart Contracts.

Smart Contracts are nothing but self-executing contracts, which execute by themselves with respect to the terms and conditions of the agreement between two parties (seller and buyer). The entire process of smart contracts is carried out with the help of lines of code. The concept of Smart Contracts dates back to as long as 1998. Smart Contracts can be tracked easily, and they are transparent as well as irreversible.

Decentralized Applications are the applications or programs that exist within a digital format in a blockchain or a P2P network, rather than just a single system. They are not under the control of a particular authority.

The main objective of Ethereum is that these smart contracts or decentralized apps can operate effectively without having any sort of downtime, fraudulent activities, control of a single authority, interference of a third party, etc.

Ethereum offers financial products accessible by any person in the world regardless of their nationality, religion, and other factors. These are considered efficient by the people who do not believe in their state or central authorities, which offer financial products such as loans, bank accounts, insurance policies, and others.

Ether is a cryptographic token, which enables an individual to acquire the services offered within Ethereum. In the general context, it is like a vehicle to explore the platform of Ethereum. All the operational activities are carried out by developers, such as the operational process of the applications in Ethereum. However, nowadays, people use Ethereum to complete transactions or buy other sorts of virtual currencies. Ether is the second-largest cryptocurrency in the world (right after Bitcoin), with a market cap of more than $199 billion, as of February 10, 2021.

In the year 2021, Ethereum changed its consensus algorithm from Proof of Work to Proof of Stake. This would help in the development of Ethereum as there will not be a requirement for a vast amount of energy or higher transaction speed.

- Litecoin (LTC):

Litecoin is among the first set of cryptocurrencies that were created. To be more specific, when Litecoin was initially invented in 2011, it was compared as silver, while Bitcoin was referred to as gold. It was created by an MIT graduate, Charlie Lee, who was a former engineer at Google. Litecoin is an open-source global payment network that is not under any sort of centralized authority.

It uses 'scrypt' as proof of work and can be decoded with the help of an average CPU that most of us use. As the block generation time of Litecoin is much faster when compared to Bitcoin, the transaction confirmation time is also much faster.

Not only are the developers for this cryptocurrency are increasing, but there has also been a significant amount of increase in the merchants that accept this cryptocurrency as a mode of payment. As of February 2021, one Litecoin is equivalent to $190.

- Ripple (XRP):

Ripple is not famous as a cryptocurrency, but it is renowned for being a digital payment network for making financial transactions. Ripple is the third-largest cryptocurrency in terms of market capitalization, right after Bitcoin and Ethereum.

Ripple's operational procedure is similar to that of SWIFT used by most of the world's major banks. This operating procedure includes payment settlement asset exchange and remittance system. Just like SWIFT, Ripple acts as a middleman in financial transactions that involve money as well as security transfers.

Ripple makes use of a consensus algorithm that involves a group of servers to confirm the transaction history. This self-made consensus algorithm of Ripple is known as Ripple Protocol Consensus Algorithm (RPCA).

The transactions on Ripple require a lesser amount of energy when compared to Bitcoin and are confirmed faster. Ripple's transaction costs are also less than that of the transactional costs of transferring money using Bitcoin. By the time of writing this book, the value of XRP is equivalent to USD 0.57.

- Tether (USDT):

Tether was a cryptocurrency that belongs to a group of cryptocurrencies known as Stablecoins. Stablecoin is a type of cryptocurrency with its value pegged to a fiat currency or any other reference point to reduce volatility. Even major cryptocurrencies such as Bitcoin have experienced significant fluctuations in their value, and therefore, cryptocurrencies such as Stablecoins try to have lesser changes. This feature alone attracts many people who are afraid to trade or invest in cryptocurrencies because of their volatility. The value of Tether is almost the same as the value of the US Dollar as Tether's value is pegged to it.

- Stellar (XLM):

Stellar is a network based on blockchain technology, which specializes in providing services to enterprises by connecting financial institutions so that they can make large transactions. Usually, when large transactions are made with banks or investment companies' help, it might take a few days and add the hefty transaction costs on top of it. However, with Stellar's help, these transactions can be made instantly, and the costs are considerably low.

Not only enterprises, but anybody can use Stellar. Cross-border transactions can be carried out using the Stellar among several currencies. Stellar has a native cryptocurrency called Lumens (XLM). To make a transaction using the Stellar network, people would have to hold Lumens. The value of one stellar by February 12, 2021, is around 0.47 (approx.).

- Cardano (ADA):

Cardano is a cryptocurrency that has been created based on research conducted by a group of mathematicians, engineers, and cryptography professionals. This project was co-founded by Charles Hoskinson, who happens to be one of the founding members of Ethereum. Cardano's primary objective is to provide decentralized financial products similar to Ethereum while concentrating on solutions for issues such as voter fraud, legal contract trading, etc.

**Honorable mentions** – Some other cryptocurrencies that are being used worldwide and worth mentioning are as follows:

- Bitcoin Cash (BCH)

- Chainlink (LINK)

- Binance Coin (BNB)

- Monero (XMR)

- Polkadot (DOT)

- Bitcoin SV (BSV)

- EOS (EOS)

- Uniswap (UNI)

- Dash (DASH)

Apart from these, there are roughly more than 4,000 cryptocurrencies in the world as of 2021.

# Chapter 11
# Cryptocurrency Trading:

**Forex Trading –** To understand what cryptocurrency trading means, we must understand the term 'Forex Trading' first. Forex is nothing but Foreign Currency Exchange, which literally means exchanging one currency for another. There are many reasons that a person would prefer to exchange currencies. Some of them are for commerce, tourism, trading, etc. It has been estimated that the average Forex trading volume worldwide was more than $5 trillion per day.

The place where people trade these foreign currencies is called a foreign exchange market. So, why would anyone need to change their currency in the first place? There is an explanation. Imagine that you live in the USA and you went to the UK on vacation. There, you wanted to buy goods, let's say, oranges. The currency used in the UK is British Pound (GBP), while your currency is the United States Dollar (USD), so how are you planning on acquiring the oranges by paying in your currency. So, when going to the UK, you will exchange the money you have with the UK's local currency. In this way, you will have the local money, which you can use to acquire goods and services in that country.
Similarly, you would need to pay in a country's specific currency for importing the goods from that country. When you are exchanging the currency, you will not get something of the exact number. For example, let us think that you wanted to exchange between USD and GBP. When you give

$10, you will not actually be receiving £10; instead, you will receive what is equivalent to $10.

There was a time when people only exchanged currencies when they were traveling to another country. These people used to exchange their home currency with the country's currency they are going to, with the help of a bank or a foreign exchange broker. Then, they would receive an amount as per the current exchange rate during that time.

Nowadays, the currency exchange is done primarily for trading, which refers to a specific type of investment trading. It is similar to trading with stocks, where the forex traders speculate the values of currencies among two different countries by doing which. Most people find it hard to gain profits while they are involved with forex trading. Let us have a look at a piece of more detailed information about forex trading and how it works.

To make it simple for you to understand, forex trading involves a currency pair consisting of two currencies: the base currency and a quote currency. For example, let us assume that you are trading with GBP and USD. Here, GBP is your base currency, and USD is the quote currency. If the GBP/USD currency pair is trading at 1.38, then it means that GBP 1 is equivalent to USD 1.38. When the value of the British Pound increases, the currency pair will increase and vice versa. When you speculate this currency pair's price to rise, you can buy the pair, which is called going long. Simultaneously, when you think that the currency pair will decrease, you can sell the pair, which is called going short. In this way, you can make profits while trading with currency pairs, and this process is known as forex trading.

**Cryptocurrency Trading** – In many aspects, people can consider cryptocurrency trading to be similar to forex trading. People can buy cryptocurrencies with the help of fiat currency such as the US Dollar, which they can trade with. They can either opt for the buy-and-hold strategy or just trade on a daily or weekly basis while making profits from the markets' volatility. People can also make money when they speculate that a specific cryptocurrency price will lose its value over time. In such cases, they can opt for future contracts or binary options.

- Future contract usually requires the trader to agree to terms that he or she will sell a specific asset at a price that has already been determined on the day that they agreed to sell. This can either result in a profit or a loss, while most traders tend to lose while investing in future contracts. This is due to the factor called leverage, where the person can trade with more money than they own.

- Options are the investment vehicles, which are derivatives based on the value of the underlying financial assets such as stocks. Options contracts offer an individual an opportunity to buy or sell their asset based on the contract that they are holding. However, if the trader chooses not to buy or sell that specific asset, they can keep it, unlike in future contracts.

- Call options allow an individual to buy an asset at a specified price within a particular timeframe. In comparison, put options allow an individual to sell an asset at a specified price within a specific timeframe. Upon the expiry of the contract, the individual holding the asset should decide on whether they are going to buy/sell it or not.

- Binary Options are financial instruments where the payout will either be a fixed amount of money or nothing at all. There are two main types of binary options, namely, the asset-or-nothing option and the cash-or-nothing option. Binary options are more like gambling rather than investment. Even many jurisdictions ban binary options as they consider binary options to be a form of gambling.

People who want to trade with cryptocurrencies can buy or sell the actual cryptocurrencies with the help of a cryptocurrency exchange, or they can just speculate the price movements using a CFD trading account.

When you want to trade with cryptocurrencies with the help of a cryptocurrency exchange, you must create an exchange account. You will be needed to deposit the entire amount of money you will buy the specific crypto asset. The cryptocurrency that you have purchased can be kept in your wallet until you feel it would be beneficial for you to sell that cryptocurrency and make money from it.

One of the most important things that are needed to be considered here is that there are certain limitations for most exchanges on particular aspects, such as how much you can deposit. Additionally, it is kind of expensive for you to maintain the accounts.

- A CFD (Contract for Difference) is a contract that pays the trader based on the differences in the price of the asset that range between the open and closing trades. Something like price bets on the assets.

- CFDs allow individuals to speculate the securities directions over a period of time and are quite famous for trading with assets such as FX and commodities.

- The payoffs on CFDs are settled in cash. However, margin trading is allowed so that an investor can only invest a small amount of the contract's actual payoff.

- People who speculate that the price is going to increase will buy a CFD. In contrast, the people who speculate a decrease in the price will sell an open position. In this way, individuals can make money on their speculations of the price movements by investing in CFDs.

Like the actual CFD trading, CFD trading on cryptocurrencies allows an individual to speculate the price movement of a cryptocurrency without actually owning that specific cryptocurrency. When you think that there will be an increase in the value of any cryptocurrency, then you can buy, which is referred to as going long. On the other hand, if you think that the value of a cryptocurrency will fall, you sell, which is referred to as going short.

Both these products are leveraged products, which means that you can make a small deposit and get full exposure to the respective underlying market. The profits or losses are calculated based on the trading position's full size, which means good becomes great and bad becomes worst.

While trading with the help of a CFD trading account, you should get familiar with some relevant terms that will come in handy for you to trade efficiently.

First of all, there is spread, which is the difference between the buy and sell prices that have been quoted for cryptocurrency trade. In general, when you want to open a long position, you will be quoted with a price that is a bit high when compared to the actual market price. Similarly, when you decide to open a short position, you will be presented with a price that is a bit low when compared with the actual market price.

Usually, cryptocurrencies are traded in lots, which are nothing but bundles of tokens of the selected cryptocurrency. This is done in order to simplify the size of trade and make them balanced. Some cryptocurrencies might be available in lots that will consist of only one unit of the actual cryptocurrencies, while some other lots might be bigger while having consistently more units.

Leverage is the method to gain broad exposure to the markets while not paying the total amount of money you are trading. For this, you will be required to pay a small amount of money called a margin. Upon closing a leveraged position, the profit or loss is determined based on the total amount of trade made. While there is a chance that you might have substantially higher amounts of profits, the risk of loss is also huge.

The margin in leveraged trading is represented in the form of a percentage of the actual full position. For example, for a $10,000 trade, let us imagine that the margin is 20%. This means you would only be required to deposit $2,000 to execute that trade. If there were profits, it would be based on the overall $10,000.

## Factors that influenced the price movements:

**In the beginning** - In the early days, people often did not have the required amount of knowledge about Bitcoin or a cryptocurrency, for that matter. This situation was responsible for the aspect that only a few investors showed interest in cryptocurrency markets. Under such circumstances, when problems such as the ban of cryptocurrencies in certain places occurred, most people panic. The increase in the price and the decrease influenced the trajectory of Bitcoin's price a lot.

Not only that, but the significant hacking events such as the one that took place at Mt. Gox were responsible for some drastic falls in the price of bitcoin.

Another major factor influencing the price movements in the early days was the acceptance of bitcoin as an actual mode of payment. To state an example, we can observe the price in 2014, when it reached more than $1,000 after an online retailer started accepting bitcoin as a payment mode.

**Current situation** – over the recent years, there is a wide range of factors that are responsible for bitcoin's price movement. When bitcoin gained a lot of attention in 2017, changes in the laws/regulations impacted the price as bitcoin started to have an extended outreach. Depending on the changes, any change in law or regulation that positively impacted the bitcoin's price led to an increase in its price and vice versa.

Interest from professional investors was one of the most crucial factors that influenced bitcoin's price significantly. As the number of investors increased, the volatility was a bit lowered because of the increased liquidity. Remarkably, most of the well-known people in the finance sector stated that money could be stored safely with the help of holding them in the form of bitcoins or any other cryptocurrencies. This would provide them safety from the inflation that might arise because of the escalated government spending during the pandemic. Even more than that, some companies even made use of bitcoin for treasury management, which positively influenced the price of bitcoin in 2020. Some notable examples of such companies that committed to bitcoin include MicroStrategy Inc. (MSTR) and Square Inc. (SQ).

The industrial sector development is also responsible for impacting bitcoin's price, especially in the tech and finance fields. After bitcoin futures trading was launched at the Cboe options exchange and Chicago Mercantile Exchange in 2017, the price reached around $20,000.

Economic instability is also a significant indicator for speculating the price changes of bitcoin. For example, we can take Venezuela as an example. When hyperinflation hit Venezuela, money was weighed for making purchases as it lost a lot of value. People of Venezuela, who have faced such extreme conditions, decided to take preventive measures to avoid such circumstances in the future. For this reason, they opted for bitcoin as a mode of payment and to store their money during the pandemic outbreak leading to an increase in the price. Therefore, it can be said that even instability in an economy can also positively influence the price movement.

**Future speculation** – Some tech and crypto experts and media intellectuals have a say in the future price prediction of bitcoin, or we can say Analysis. As discussed, bitcoin has crossed more than $50,000, and financial news providers such as 'Fortune' say that the markets will still be bullish.

In 2014, specifically when a bitcoin's price was around $623, a Stanford economist, Susan Athey, stated that there is a possibility for bitcoin to reach $50,000 in the future. Yeah, predictions are natural, and almost many people's predictions come true (based on the probability of true or false). This is not an instance that can be predicted by most people, though. Most of the people who were even the loyal fans of bitcoin did not dare to utter such predictions. They just had awe for a lot of time seeing $20,000 in 2017 and thought it could be the all-time highest.

Even the people who indeed predicted such a massive surge in the price movement are wrong to think so. Why? We can get our answer for that from Susan's assessment of potential future bitcoin prices.

Keeping all the needless data aside, we must concentrate on that Susan, and other bullish thinkers stated that positive influence on the price of bitcoin would come from the theory of demand and supply. That is not the actual case here, and we can prove this with the help of practical technical barriers.

Bitcoin has not been an ideal mode of payment, defeating the primary purpose here. Of course, it has seen a growth relevant to remittances, but this alone will not be enough to impact the price movement.

The major reason is not even the Venezuelans, most of who opted for bitcoin during last year. The major reason behind the huge increase, as much as $50,000, is due to Tesla. How is an electric vehicle manufacturer responsible for influencing the price of a decentralized cryptocurrency? It is not because that they have any connection or something. The actual reason is that Tesla invested around $1.5 billion in bitcoin in February 2021. This is the final push given to bitcoin's price, which made it have such a significant amount of increase.

What would tesla do with $1.5 billion worth of bitcoins, especially when the company itself has a market cap of around $685.82? The critical reason corporate giants such as Tesla came forward to make an investment in Bitcoin is to store the value. This started in 2017. What would a company such as Tesla by storing the value of a tiny amount of $1.5 billion (little compared to their market cap)? Tesla will not be using that money for making payments at a coffee shop or a grocery store. Instead, they want to use it in the form of a bank account as bitcoin is not connected with any other assets or is not controlled by any monetary authority. The rapid growth of investors will either increase the price of bitcoin or maintain it steadily.

# Chapter 12
# Working procedure of a Bitcoin:

Having read about the operational procedure of cryptocurrency, it would not be hard now for you to understand the working process of a bitcoin. To revise the information, we will just have a brief look at how a bitcoin works.

Bitcoin is a file with the data related to your transaction or receipt, which has an actual value. We can divide it into three parts to have a better understanding. They are transaction input, transaction output, and the amount.

So, when you buy a bitcoin, you are not just pulling it out of thin air. It was sent to you from a particular place known as a bitcoin address. Here, the bitcoin address from which the payment or transaction has been made (source) would be referred to as transaction input. The bitcoin address to which the payment or transaction has been made (destination) would be called a transaction output.

When you send a bitcoin to somebody else, your wallet will create a transaction output. This transaction output is nothing but the bitcoin address to which you are sending the funds. In that transaction, as the bitcoin has been transferred from your account, your bitcoin address will be registered as transaction input. Simultaneously, when the person who received the bitcoin sends it to another person, their address will become the transaction input. The address of the third person who received the bitcoin will ultimately be the transaction output. As for the amount, we think there is no need for much of an explanation.

With this system's help, people could track bitcoin transactions up to the time when the first-ever bitcoin was created. This would help them by providing detailed information about the transactions.

However, the amount involved with the transactions is not divisible. Let us see an example. Imagine two persons, namely A and B, where A wants to send half a bitcoin to B. when A tries to send that half bitcoin, A would have to send that entire bitcoin and then get half bitcoin in change from the network. This change will be sent back to A in a third address, which will also be considered a transaction output. Therefore, bitcoin transactions would typically consist of many transaction outputs. As a result of this, the wallets comprise many bitcoins addresses with varying amounts and changes from the transactions made.

When a person sends a bitcoin to someone, the wallet of that person will try mostly to piece the required funds together with the help of addresses containing different amounts. Therefore, there will be transactions with many different inputs, various bitcoin addresses, and different amounts to make up for the funds. Considering all these factors, you might end up with change as these inputs won't necessarily be able to deliver the exact amounts.

While talking about bitcoin, bitcoin can be sent in smaller amounts such as mBTC and satoshis, while satoshis are the least. As we know, satoshis are the 100 millionth part of a bitcoin, which is a small fraction of a dollar, which is around 0.00049. However, when transactions are made in much smaller amounts, the whole network would be clogged with numerous tiny transactions. To keep that in check, the smallest transaction that can be made using bitcoin would have a limit of around 546 satoshis, which is also considerably low.

Adding to that, almost all the transactions made using bitcoin would have a transaction fee. Hence, when you want to send a bitcoin to somebody, you would have to send an additional amount to make up for the transaction costs involved. If transaction costs are not covered, the chances for the transaction to fail are highly likely. This should be carefully considered, especially while making bitcoin transactions using smaller amounts.

Hence, when you are using a bitcoin wallet and have successfully made a few transactions, you will start seeing various bitcoin addresses with a lot of tiny amounts. You now understand why.

# **Chapter 13**
# **Transactions Process of Bitcoin:**

The transaction process of bitcoin is based on the blockchain system, which we have discussed earlier in our book. The transaction process is the most important thing while understanding a bitcoin. Everything about bitcoin is associated with transactions to make sure that the transactions can be created, propagated on the network, validated, and added to the blockchain. Transactions are nothing but the data that encodes the transfer between individuals in the bitcoin network. Each and every transaction made using bitcoin is a public entry on the blockchain, which is the global ledger.

**Transaction lifecycle –** We know about nodes, blockchain, and miners so far. Now, it will be quite easy for us to understand the transaction lifecycle of bitcoin. To briefly say, the transaction lifecycle consists of the following steps.

- Transaction life cycle starts with creating a transaction, which might also be referred to as an origination.

- The transaction is then signed with necessary signatures, which can be one or more. This will help in the authorization of spending the funds by referencing the transaction.

- This transaction will then be broadcasted onto the bitcoin network, where each node would have to validate the transaction making sure that it is okay.

- This process is carried out by all the nodes on the blockchain until all the nodes have successfully verified the transaction.

- In the end, the transaction would be verified with the help of a mining node and will be included in a block, which would be added to the blockchain.

After the transaction has been recorded on the blockchain and enough blocks confirm it, the transaction becomes a permanent part of the bitcoin ledger. It would be accepted as a valid transaction by all the participants. After that, the recipient's funds can be used for another transaction, and then the transaction life cycle would start again.

An example transaction of a bitcoin would appear something like this:

15N3xGu3UFHeyUNdzQ6sS4aRFRzy5Ay7RZ sent 0.0256742 bitcoin to 1JHG2ghdk5Khik7X5xQrr1wwtgepJEK4t on February 19 between 11:10 and 11:20 a.m.

Here, the strings that contain numbers and alphabets are the bitcoin addresses.

**Bitcoin mining** – We have discussed what miners do, but we have not discussed miners or the process of mining in detail. So, we will now present a clear and detailed view of the mining process.

The process of bitcoin mining takes a lot of time, effort, and money. And for all that, the people who are involved with the mining process would be paid a reward occasionally. Even though people tend to become miners so that they can get that reward, which is usually paid out to them as a fraction of bitcoin.

Literally, people involved with the mining process can acquire bitcoin without actually having to pay for it.

For each and every block that has been added to the blockchain, the miners would be paid a reward.

However, not all the miners involved with the mining process will be getting a reward for what they do. Moreover, the miner who discovered the solution to a complex hashing puzzle first will be rewarded.

The chances of miners getting a reward will depend on the portion of the miner's total mining power on the network.

To carry out the mining process, miners would need a GPU (Graphics Processing Unit) or an Application Specific Integrated Circuit (ASIC).

Great! Do you want to become a miner so that you can also try to get rewarded? But before hastily doing so, here is some key information that will come in handy for you or change your mind.

The rewarding process is done to attract more miners to the bitcoin network. By doing so, the bitcoin network, which is decentralized, can be made legit by tracking the transactions and ensuring whether those transactions are valid or not. Just mainly because of these miners, Bitcoin can work independently by not relying on any of the monetary authorities.

Miners can be considered more auditors, as they are verifying the legitimacy of the transactions. By verifying the transactions, the double-spending problem of bitcoin can be kept in check.

After verifying transactions sizing around 1MB, which is also called a block, the miners will be rewarded with a fraction of bitcoin. Satoshi Nakamoto has set this limit of 1MB. Most people say that increasing this limit would help accommodate more data and efficiently carry out the process faster than usual.

Yes, miners who have verified 1MB of transactions would be rewarded, but everyone would be rewarded. To do so, the miner would have to do it before all other miners. So, if you become a miner, the chances of getting rewarded are not in your favour, as you would have to solve a numeric problem first.

Miners will not need to have advanced math skills or high-level computation. To become the first miner to be rewarded, you need to come up with a 64-digit hexadecimal number known as a hash. It is just guesswork.

Regardless of just being guesswork, the total number of possible guesses for these problems can be trillions. For this, miners require a lot of computing power, which is precisely a high hash rate and is measured in megahashes (MH/s) per second, gigahashes per second (GH/s), and terahashes per second (TH/s).

Mining attracts new miners and helps maintain the bitcoin ecosystem and is also helpful in releasing new bitcoins into circulation. Aside from the coins created using the genesis block, which happens to be the first block on the bitcoin network, every other bitcoin came into existence because of the miners. Without miners, there will not be any additional bitcoins released into circulation. There will be a time when bitcoin mining would come to an end for creating new bitcoins. This would be when the last bitcoin of all the 21 million bitcoins comes into circulation.

Won't there be any work for bitcoin miners after all the bitcoins come into circulation? That is not true. Even after all the bitcoins come into circulation, miners are necessary to verify the transactions, and for that, they will be paid in fees that have been acquired in the form of transaction costs.

Miners are also offered voting power, which can be utilized while making new Bitcoin protocol changes.

The reward amount that is given to a miner is reduced by half after every four years. When bitcoin was introduced in the year 2009, mining a block would generate a reward of 50 bitcoins. This was halved to 25 BTC in 2012, 12.5 BTC in 2016, and finally is at 6.25 BTC since 2020.

In the early days, the mining process was straightforward, and people could mine with the help of an ordinary computer. The difficulty of solving a puzzle increases over time and needs increased computing power. To effectively carry out the process of verifying the transactions, the Bitcoin network is required to have one block produced every 10 minutes. If there are 1 million mining rigs in the world, then there would be ten mining rigs working on the same problem at a time. When the computing power is increased, the difficulty level of mining also gets increased for keeping the block production at a stable rate. When launched in the year 2009, the difficulty level was 1, while it is more than 20.6 trillion now because of the increased number of miners.

Therefore, to carry out the mining process in an efficient way, miners need to get their hands-on robust equipment such as GPU or ASIC, which would cost them $500 to thousands of dollars. Some miners try to buy various GPUs so that they can cut down the costs involved.

Didn't quite understand about the hash puzzle and all? Well, think that there are three persons, namely Michael, Bruce, and Jack, if Jack wrote a number on a paper between 1 to 10 and wanted Bruce and Michael to find that number. Jack sets a condition, saying that each person will get one chance at a time for guessing, and the winner will be rewarded. Then, Bruce or Michael will try and find the number, which was thought of by jack. Similarly, the person to solve the hash puzzle gets rewarded, except for the fact that all the miners working to solve a block will do that at the same time. Here, the miner would have to guess a hexadecimal number of 64 digits. Hence, it becomes tough to find the exact answer.

If Bruce and Michael were to write that answer on a piece of paper one at a time and both were right, the condition is that the first person to guess would be rewarded, then the person who gets the correct guess before the other wins. Similarly, among the miners involved in solving a puzzle, the first miner to solve it would get the reward.

Why do we have to deal with these 64-digit hexadecimal numbers while mining bitcoins? Remember the number jack wrote on a paper? Similarly, something called a target hash will be undisclosed in the process of bitcoin mining. What miners are doing exactly is that they are making random guesses of this target hash. Each guess is referred to as a nonce, which is abbreviated as number used only once. This nonce is the key for generating the hash and has a size of 32 bits. To increase the chances of getting rewarded, miners often form groups known as mining pools and share the reward in between them.

# Chapter 14
# Where can I buy Bitcoin and Cryptocurrencies?

**Cryptocurrency Exchange** – You can either own a bitcoin or trade with it just like you do in the case of stocks. To buy or sell a bitcoin, you would require access to a bitcoin exchange.

A bitcoin exchange is nothing but a digital platform that can convert fiat currencies into bitcoin or any other cryptocurrency. Each individual cryptocurrency exchange has varied prices and platforms, which allow you to deposit money and convert it into a cryptocurrency.

In general, cryptocurrency exchanges act as a middleman between the people who want to buy cryptocurrencies and the people who want to sell them. If you buy a bitcoin wallet, the transactions are recorded on the blockchain. Most of the exchanges allow you to make transactions without needing you to have a wallet.

Bitcoin exchanges are entirely legal in the United States. However, you would have to do some research on which exchange might be beneficial for you according to your requirements.

There are some influential factors for selecting the best cryptocurrency exchange. Some of these main factors include security, costs, accessibility, funding sources, etc. Some of the best cryptocurrency exchanges where you can buy bitcoin are given below.

- Coinbase:

There is no doubt that Coinbase happens to be one of the best places to buy bitcoin. Moreover, it happens to be the best option for beginners to buy bitcoin as it supports many cryptocurrencies, has a good track record, and minimum fees.

Coinbase has more than 43 million users in the United States and has a substantially long track record. Most of the assets available in Coinbase are securely stored offline in cold storage/cold wallet.

Spread is somewhat high, and the relevant fees are high for the transactions made with debit cards.

- eToro:

eToro is particularly good for beginners as it has an easy-to-use platform and even provides demo accounts for the practice. Along with that, there is a feature known as copy-trading, which allows you to copy other people's trading activity.

However, eToro has a spread of 0.75% for buying bitcoin and even higher fees for some other cryptocurrencies.

- Robinhood:

Robinhood is a cost-efficient way of buying bitcoin, and it offers commission-free trades on bitcoin. The platform of Robinhood is quite easy to understand as it is similar to that of a stock trading platform.

Not many types of cryptocurrencies can be accessed with the help of Robinhood, and the bitcoin that has been purchased cannot be transferred to a bitcoin wallet.

- Coinmama:

Bitcoins can be instantly purchased with the help of Coinmama, can be transferred to a wallet after purchasing. The account setup and accessibility are good while having a lot of options for funding.

The fee structure at Coinmama to buy bitcoin is complex, and an additional fee of 5% is applicable for buying instantly. ACH bank transfers are not allowed within Coinmama.

- BlockFi:

BlockFi is another option for buying bitcoin, which is considered one of the best. Why are we saying so? Here is why. When you buy bitcoin using BlockFi, you can deposit it into an interest-earning account, which pays you up to 8.6%.

The bitcoins you have purchased can be used to acquire a loan by keeping those very bitcoins as collateral. There are no fees for trading with cryptocurrencies with the help of BlockFi.

However, the interest rates for loans can be remarkably high and range up to 9.3%.

**HODLling** – One moment. HODLing? No, we didn't spell it wrong. In the terminology related to cryptocurrencies, HODLing is the process where a person buys and holds on to a cryptocurrency instead of selling it within a short period of time.

Most people tend to use this buy-and-hold strategy for bitcoins, and the reason, as we know, it is the increase in the price. Bitcoin tends to be a good sort of investment available to the people nowadays, and the HODLing will be more advantageous.

# Chapter 15
# Taxes and Scams

**Taxes** – In the United States, Bitcoin is considered an asset just like any other asset, and therefore, people who own bitcoins would be required to pay taxes.

The amount made by buying and selling bitcoins is liable for capital gains tax. If bitcoins are owned for less than a year before selling them, short-term capital gains apply, and for more than a year, long-term capital gains apply.

If a person has been paid in bitcoin for the goods or services he rendered, he would have to pay taxes as per the market value during the time he received them.

**Scams involved** – As there are more chances of gaining money with bitcoin, new investors started to pay more attention to bitcoin. Especially, people who might not be familiar with everything about bitcoin might want to invest in it and make money. Such people are the best suitable targets for cybercriminals, such as con artists, hackers, and scammers. Because bitcoin is not regulated by any monetary authority, the chances of fraudulent activities and the possibility for crime have increased. Given below are some of the most popular types of scams that you need to aware of.

- Fake Bitcoin Exchange:

There are some fake Bitcoin Exchanges, which take people's money and disappear. In the year 2017, a fake cryptocurrency exchange named BitKRX was exposed by the South Koran financial authorities. Even the local bitcoin community helped from their part to expose this phony exchange.

- Ponzi Scheme:

Ponzi Scheme is a scheme where a person takes money from investors and uses it to pay the previous investors from whom he took the money. This can apply to bitcoin as well, and there was an incident related to this. In 2019, 3 men were arrested for doing such a pyramid scheme with bitcoin and other cryptocurrencies. This fraudulent activity was known to be worth around $722 million.

- Fake cryptocurrencies:

Always try to trade or invest in the cryptocurrencies that have been in the market for quite some time. New cryptocurrencies might look beneficial, but the risks involved with them are heavy. Some people tell the name of a new cryptocurrency and ask you to invest to profit from it after its price increase. You should never invest or buy that cryptocurrency in such cases as there will not be any guarantee that it will be there continuously or not.

- Traditional Scams:

There are many instances where scammers call people and say that they are from a monetary authority. They continue by saying that you owe them money in the form of taxes, which need to be paid right away. Most people might be aware of such scams, but some people pay by trusting those scammers. You should never make a hasty payment as monetary authorities will not ask for payments by doing so.

- Malware:

Malware is the most commonly used method to get hold of a person's password. It can be used to get all the necessary information such as bank details, credit card information, etc., which is now being used to gain access to the bitcoin wallet credentials. Never click on any suspicious emails or links, as this is the only way malware can attack your system or device.

# Chapter 16
# Pros & Cons:

The advantages and disadvantages are pretty much the same as those of cryptocurrencies. Therefore, we shall have a brief look again comparing other cryptocurrencies so that you can be aware of what are the benefits you get and what are the caveats when you are dealing with bitcoin.

**Pros** – First, the advantages:

- Greater Liquidity:

Bitcoin has more liquidity, even when compared to other cryptocurrencies. Therefore, people who want to convert bitcoin to fiat currencies can do so without losing most of its value. The case is not the same for other cryptocurrencies as they cannot be changed directly into fiat currencies, or they lose some of their inherent value while being converted.

This makes bitcoin similar to a fiat currency rather than a cryptocurrency. However, there are some limits on how much can be bought at a particular time, which might also be observed while looking at major currencies such as the US Dollar.

- Acceptance:

As days pass, Bitcoin is has become liked by many people, and the number of merchants that accept Bitcoin as a mode of payment is increasing. Because of help from websites like Overstock.com, people can now buy many things online using bitcoins. Along with that, Bitcoin is the only cryptocurrency that has gained such popularity in contrast to its peers.

- Easy transaction process:

Bitcoin has made it easy for people to make international transactions easily, even when compared to making transactions using fiat currencies. There are no additional fees for making international transactions or any limits in doing so. This can be done easily, just like making payments or transfers using a credit card or international money transfers. However, international credit card transfers, or ATM fees can be around 3% of the transaction amount or higher than that. Not only that, but money transfer fees range up to 15%, which is considerably a lot.

Other cryptocurrencies might not have the ability to make international payments or transfers as they are not as popular as Bitcoin.

- Low fees:

Not just international transfer fees, but the overall transaction costs of Bitcoin are comparatively low. They are even lower than the transaction fees of credit cards or e-Wallets such as PayPal. These payment modes may charge around 2% to 5% of the transaction amount as a transaction fee, while the transaction fees for bitcoin rarely go over 1%.

- Anonymity and Privacy:

Having fiat currencies in a bank and using them for executing payments or transfers is not an activity that will safeguard your privacy. Even though the bank accounts are protected from various kinds of cyber-attacks, data regarding your spending and how much you receive can be tracked by monetary authorities or private merchants.

When people opt for bitcoin, they can separate their Bitcoin accounts from their public profile if they want to. It is possible to track transactions using bitcoin addresses, but it becomes difficult to track the people who have those addresses.

- Independence:

Bitcoin is a currency, which monetary authorities or governments cannot create, and neither can it be controlled by such authorities. As it is not related to any political system, governments or any other authorities cannot freeze the funds or seize the units. Whether it is a criminal investigation or a political act, the funds cannot be taken away from a person.

As bitcoin is decentralized, popular, and has greater liquidity, it is free from its creators' moral obligation. Most other cryptocurrencies are characterized based on their concentrated holdings, which means that most of those cryptocurrencies are held within a few accounts. This allows the creators of other cryptocurrencies to manipulate the supply and value, which impacts the holders.

- Built-in scarcity:

As we know it and have read about it a lot in this book, Bitcoin has a limit of 21 million units. After 21 million units of bitcoin have been created, there won't be anymore. When the supply becomes less, demand becomes more, which is the same for bitcoin as well. Some other cryptocurrencies, such as Dogecoin, are not that scarce, making them take a long time (decades) to increase the price.

Because of the built-in scarcity, bitcoin can be like that of gold and other precious metals when it comes to intrinsic value.

- Reduced risk of Inflation:

In contrast to the fiat currencies in the world, which are created and controlled by governments and local authorities, Bitcoin is free from inflation. Even though we can see many fluctuations in the price of bitcoin, there will definitely be a price hike in the long term.

- Easy to trade:

Stock trading necessitates a person to hold a certificate or license. The people who want to trade with stocks would also have to get access to a broker for doing so. Bitcoin trading, on the other hand, is not like that. In fact, it is easy. You can buy or sell a bitcoin with a bitcoin exchange and store them in a bitcoin wallet. As simple as that.

**Cons:**

Now, the bad part:

- Scams and Frauds:

Even though bitcoin is the primary cryptocurrency globally, it has experienced a lot of scams, frauds, and cyber-attacks. There have been things on a smaller level, such as Ponzi schemes, to a massive level such as hacks (one that took place at Mt. Gox).

Most other cryptocurrencies do not have as many users as Bitcoin, and therefore, they are less likely to be targeted by cybercriminals. When such things happen in a centralized system, governments or monetary authorities take the necessary action, but that does not happen with bitcoin.

- Black Market activity:

Bitcoin is a good option for people who want to maintain their privacy and anonymity. But here, criminals also maintain their privacy and anonymity with the help of bitcoin. Bitcoin is being used on the dark web and deep web for illegal activities and frauds. If this keeps continuing, Bitcoin will get a bad reputation in the future.

- High volatility:

Let us face it. Bitcoin is the cryptocurrency, which is considered to have greater liquidity when compared to other cryptocurrencies. Even though it remains a volatile asset with huge swings in its value over a short period of time, these swings can be beneficial for short-term traders, while people who are in it for the long run might sometimes panic and withdraw their funds at a loss.

- No refunds:

This is a considerable drawback of bitcoin among all other disadvantages. Bitcoin does not have a policy for refunds or chargebacks, which is devastating. If the funds have been sent to the wrong address or if the amount has been sent accidentally, then bye-bye Bitcoin.

However, cryptocurrencies such as Ripple are now implementing a policy for chargebacks and refunds. Therefore, soon, there might be a slight possibility that we might be seeing such a policy in bitcoin as well.

- Can be replaced:

Bitcoin was and still is the best cryptocurrency in the world, but the question is, will it continue to be that way?

What if any other cryptocurrency, let us say Litecoin, had an increase in its value and exceeded bitcoin? Then Litecoin would become the best cryptocurrency in the world. Nowadays, there are many cryptocurrencies that have the same structure as Bitcoin but are implementing even more features than it.

There have been new cryptocurrencies with features such as increased privacy, smart contracts, in-house exchange, etc. If people get attracted to these types of features and start paying more attention to them, bitcoin might lose its value.

- Mining issues (environmental):

Bitcoin mining requires a lot of electricity and equipment, for which only one miner would be rewarded. This is a bit inconvenient.

Along with that, most of the bitcoin mining companies are based in China, where the power is generated from coal plants. The smog created from these plants will be harmful to the people who are living around and be a factor in the already increased pollution in the world.

Anyhow, we might be seeing a lot of clean energy projects in the future, which will reduce the environmental impact.

- Limited use:

The primary reason for the creation of Bitcoin was to make transactions online. However, people these days are using it only for trading and storing it as a form of investment. Adding to that, bitcoin is currently being accepted by a few merchants all over the world.

- Possibility of loss:

If the wallet is a hardware wallet, and the wallet crashes, the person cannot access their bitcoins. Not only hardware wallets, but even web, mobile, and desktop wallets also come with the problem of being lost if there is a virus or the system crashes.

- Government regulations:

The Indian government is trying to ban cryptocurrencies and is trying to implement this idea. In a short time, India will ban its people from investing or trading with cryptocurrencies. This is a devastating thing for India's people, who have invested a lot of amount in Bitcoin and are waiting for profits in the long run. Countries such as Algeria, Saudi Arabia, Qatar, Vietnam have imposed a ban on cryptocurrencies and consider it illegal to get involved in relevant activities.

Similarly, if any other country will also develop such regulations for maintaining value to their centralized currencies, bitcoin will systematically lose its value.

# Final Word:

Bitcoin is the most successful cryptocurrency globally, with a considerable increase in its value over recent years. Keeping the demand and supply theory in mind, as it becomes scarce, it will see many surges in its price. However, we should also look at the downsides of it before getting into the deal. Suppose other countries of the world also follow the ideology of countries such as Qatar, Vietnam, Saudi Arabia, Algeria, Bolivia, etc., which currently have a ban on cryptocurrencies. In that case, the value of bitcoin will be affected a lot. Not only that, but the people who have invested a lot of money in cryptocurrencies might have to lose their money unless they are at a profit right now.

On the bright side, bitcoin is nothing less than precious metals such as gold when it comes to having intrinsic value or any other real money characteristics. The thing about bitcoin is ironic as it has all the essential attributes of legit money, yet it does not even exist.

Bitcoin can be utilized for beating inflation, maintaining privacy, or executing transactions at lower costs. Many advantages make bitcoin one of the best forms of money that exists in our world. As the days pass by, more and more people are becoming attracted to cryptocurrencies, and acceptability is seeing a lot of increase worldwide.

We hope you enjoyed reading this book and hope you could learn everything you need to understand bitcoin more clearly. Thanks for reading this book, and we wish you the absolute best for your future if you are thinking about investing in Bitcoin and cryptocurrency.

CPSIA information can be obtained
at www.ICGtesting.com
Printed in the USA
LVHW110311310122
709822LV00007B/31